DELIGHT
in the art of
Collage

LISA M. PACE

NORTH LIGHT BOOKS

Cincinnati, Ohio

www.artistsnetwork.com

Contents

Sunshine surrounds the earth as surrounds our souls.

Terri Guillemets

6

Introduction

Not only do I take delight in techniques used in my projects, but I also take delight in the assemblage of these projects. Starting with a blank canvas, then adding and adding to create a mixed-media project or piece of collage art with my very own hands is something I find so rewarding. I'm often asked how I created a piece, where I get my inspiration and if I have any helpful hints I can share. So I thought it would be fun to write a book that showcases just that—how to put everything together to create amazing projects using current and vintage finds. In this book, I not only share with you step-by-step techniques but also lead you through the extra steps necessary to get the end result—my projects are explained from start to finish. Each project is perfect to keep for your very own or to give as gifts. And you know each one will have that endearing vintage charm that I love so much.

The projects in this book show you how to incorporate vintage finds like old buttons, sewing patterns, metal spoons, tart tins, fabric remnants, trims and so much more. I find these items during my travels or just digging around booths at flea markets, antique stores or thrift shops. I never tire of the hunt for treasures, and it is common to see me getting down and dirty, scraping off layers of grime from metal pieces or scrubbing soiled linens or fabrics. I see nothing but beauty in all things stained, tattered, torn and rusted.

In Chapter One, you will find unique ways to use textiles of all sorts. I'll introduce you to the art of needle felting, show you how to create a beautiful dahlia from a tattered quilt, and print treasured family photos onto muslin. Chapter Two is all about metal. You will learn how to turn an empty soda can into a beautiful flower to use as the focal point on a canvas, as well as how to stamp onto metal to create charms to use as embellishments on projects. In Chapter Three, you will use melt art mediums as well as resin, clay and embossing powders. This chapter features techniques like creating faux handblown glass tiles from embossing enamel and creating a faux enameled patina effect using embossing powders. Chapter Four is filled with projects using all kinds of paper, from vintage sheet music and ledger paper to sewing patterns and patterned papers. You will learn how to fashion beautiful feather embellishments from old book pages and silhouettes from family photos. You will also see how easy it is to create beautiful resin paper butterflies that accent a three-dimensional canvas piece.

My two wishes for you are to enjoy the creative process from start to finish and to look beyond the item. Just because it is a canvas does not mean it has to remain just that. Turn it around and use the back to create a shadow box or body for a doll. A beautiful vintage platter can easily become the canvas for a family photo accented with buttons and trims. Tart tins and gelatin molds aren't just for baking—they can be stacked together to create amazing flowers. So when you look at an object, try to think of a way to use it other than its original purpose. This kind of discovery is a fun part of the creative journey that you do not want to miss out on.

About the Materials Lists

The techniques in this book each include a list of the general materials you will need to accomplish that technique. For a complete list of the exact materials I used to make the projects shown, see pages 119–123.

Chapter One
Textiles

If you want to see me get a little skip in my step, just throw a bunch of vintage feed sacks, dish towels, fabric remnants, lace and trims into a basket and toss it on a table. When I spot a basket like this at a flea market, I cannot get there fast enough. It is so fun digging through all these goodies. I tell you, it's the thrill of the hunt that gets me every time, and I come by it honestly because my mom and dad love the hunt as much as I do. Just remember: It can be washed; stains are OK and create a distressed feel; and tattered and torn is good. But most importantly—if you like it, buy it. This chapter is filled with creative ways to use all those textile finds you come upon during your shopping adventures. You will assemble a textile charm using remnant pieces of canvas and lace and adorned with a basic needle-felted accent, and you will create a unique doll using a sewing pattern for her skirt that is accented beautifully with trim and seam binding.

Bird's Nest

This collage highlights meaningful items from a place I love to visit. For the past several summers, I've driven with my parents to West Virginia to visit family and the old homestead. This homestead was placed in its spot in 1900, so I used a postcard and sheet music from that era for my background. The wallpaper is pieces of the home's actual wallpaper, which Mom and I carefully peeled away. The buttons and chenille bedspread nest represent items found in the attic. The ladle symbolizes all the wonderful meals my great-great-aunts cooked on a woodstove.

What You'll Need

Ladle, chenille fabric, crochet trim, yarn, embroidery floss, beads for eggs, daisy trim, buttons, fabric leaf, small chandelier beads, hot glue sticks, hot glue gun, sewing needle, scissors

1 Using scissors, cut pieces of a chenille bedspread or fabric, yarn and crochet trim to 1" × 12" (3cm × 30cm). Hold all three pieces together and tie a knot at one end.

2 Starting at the knotted end, twist the textiles together to form a nest shape. Using a hot glue gun, apply small dots of hot glue to the top of the textiles strip before you layer the next twisted row. This will help keep the nest's shape as it gets larger. Add additional dots of glue as needed, one or two per row. Glue the ends of the fabric to the nest to secure.

3 Wrap a bit of yarn around the nest, working bottom to top, to add body and visual interest, gluing both ends of the yarn in place.

4 Using a sewing needle or hot glue gun, attach three beads to the center of the nest for eggs.

5 To complete the nest, add vintage buttons, small felt leaves and flower trim. You can either sew them on or attach them with hot glue. For additional texture, attach the small chandelier beads with embroidery floss. Double knot the floss ends and leave the strings hanging.

6 Adhere the nest to the bowl of the ladle with hot glue.

To finish this project, hot glue an old earring, additional leaves and a seam binding bow to the handle of the ladle. Cover a 7" × 9" (18cm × 23cm) canvas with patterned papers. Adhere the Dresden trim to the top and bottom edges. Hot glue the ladle to the canvas, then continue to embellish the canvas with buttons, beads and game tiles. You can sew the beads to the velvet ribbon, if you like, but attach the rest of the items with hot glue.

Felted Heart

I wanted the background for this piece to be pretty much all cream colored so the main focus would fall on the felted heart. Different textiles, such as lace, wool felt and doilies, in similar colors help create a lovely monochromatic theme. Adding cream pearls and vintage buttons for accents provides dimension and texture. The hand stitching in the heart and on the other accent items ties the whole piece together.

What You'll Need

Zipper, wool felt, wool roving in two colors, embroidery floss, beads, pencil, embroidery needle, needle-felting pen, brush needle-felting pad, scissors

1 Trim the fabric part of your zipper as close to the zipper teeth as you can with scissors.

2 With a pencil, lightly draw the shape of your heart onto cream felt, adding some circles to accent with a second color of wool roving.

3 Using an embroidery needle threaded with cream embroidery floss, begin sewing the zipper trim onto the pencil lines. Stitch in an up-and-over motion, sewing between each tooth of the zipper.

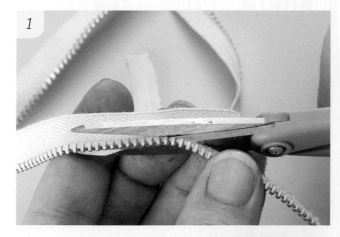

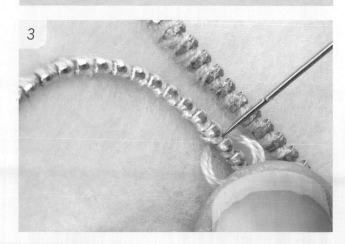

4 Place your felt piece onto a brush-style needle-felting pad. Pull off a piece of cream wool roving; do not cut the roving. When pulling off pieces of roving, hold the roving at one end with one hand and gently pull the roving with the other hand from the opposite end. It will pull apart like cotton candy.

5 Place the roving in the heart. Using a pen-style needle-felting tool, press the needles into the wool roving. The barbs on the needle will attach the wool roving to the felt and compact the roving. Continue until the wool roving fills the heart shape up to the edge of the zipper teeth.

6 Accent the circles with the second color of roving.

7 Use embroidery floss to hand stitch areas with simple straight stitches.

8 Add rice grain stitches. To create this stitch, sew a single basic straight stitch at any angle, and continue creating single straight stitches of similar size randomly at different angles until the area is filled. When finished, the rice stitches should resemble that of spilled rice, with the rice pieces going in all different directions.

9 Hand stitch small beads inside the heart for additional accents.

10 Carefully cut the felt as close to the zipper teeth as possible, making sure not to cut any of the stitching.

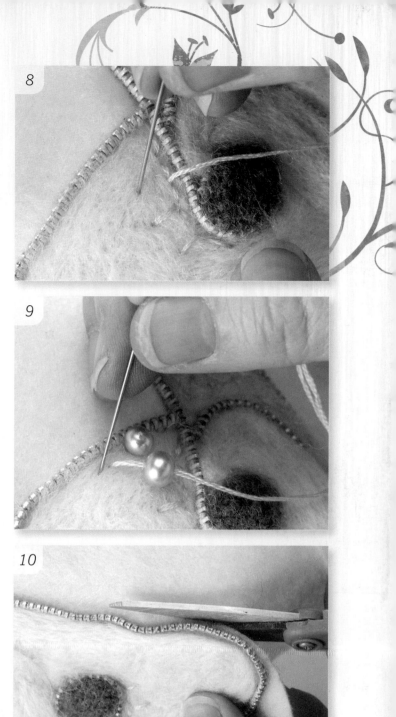

To finish this project, wrap a 5" × 5" (13cm × 13cm) canvas with felt, and glue the felt to the back of the canvas. Adhere lace over the felt by sewing or with fabric adhesive. Place a second layer of lace over the first, then use fabric adhesive to attach the heart embellishment. Stitch on buttons and beads as desired. Hand stitch a message, such as *peace*, to a piece of muslin. Trim the muslin, and sew or glue it to the lace.

Textile Cuff

The items I cannot pass up when treasure hunting are broken necklaces, tattered doilies, shell or glass buttons, quilt scraps, earrings and other like items. These castoffs add a unique charm to anything I make, and to me there is no better creative feeling than turning a discarded item into beautiful wearable art and one-of-a-kind jewelry, like this textile cuff. I love making and wearing textile cuffs with my everyday attire or for a night on the town.

What You'll Need

Quilt pieces or alterable cuff, lace trim, crocheted doily, textile flower, rhinestone trim, pearl bead chain, buttons, baker's twine, thread, embroidery floss, fabric adhesive, sewing needle

1 To create the base for your cuff, cut two pieces of quilt to 1½" × 8½" (4cm × 22cm), or use a purchased alterable cuff. Set aside the piece for the back of the cuff. Sew trim to the long edges of the top piece, or attach the trim using fabric adhesive.

2 Sew the textile flower to the center of the top cuff piece or attach with fabric adhesive. Accent the flower with a clear glass button. Cut a small crocheted doily in half and attach it to the cuff using fabric adhesive.

3 Sew buttons randomly to both sides of the flower or use fabric adhesive, if you prefer.

4 Sew rhinestone trim to the long edges of the cuff, placing one on the upper right edge and one on lower left edge. Sew a strand of pearl bead chain to each side of the textile flower.

5 Sew a button onto one end of the cuff; this will be part of the closure.

6 Using fabric adhesive, attach the second strip of the cuff to the back of the altered cuff. Before you close up the end opposite the closure button, create a loop with baker's twine and insert it between the two layers. Add additional glue, if needed.

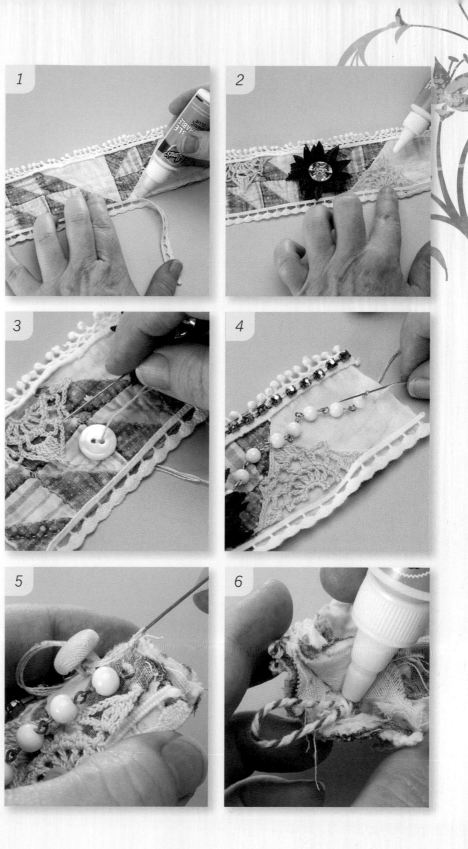

Tip

If you do not want a button closure, you can create a bow-type closure. Sandwich a piece of seam binding between the two layers of the cuff, leaving enough seam binding at each end to tie a bow.

Assemblage Charm

This charm is layered with a doily I cut from a tattered table runner and a canvas piece I cut from an old tote. I wanted to ground the piece, so I added a felted black circle. It helps accent the vintage buttons since everything else is in an ecru color scheme. I really don't worry about mixing gold, copper and silver. I like the eclectic feel that comes across when all of these are used together. Attach the charm to pearl bead chain or rosary-style beads or a link-style chain.

What You'll Need

Canvas fabric, burlap, lace trim, wool roving, two buttons in graduated sizes, three eyelets, embroidery floss, fabric adhesive, hot glue sticks, hot glue gun, sewing needle, scissors, needle-felting pen, brush needle-felting pad, Crop-A-Dile tool

1 Cut a piece of canvas to 1½" × 1½" (4cm × 4cm). Cut a piece of burlap into a square slightly smaller than 1½" (4cm). Using fabric adhesive, attach the burlap to the canvas, then glue a piece of lace trim to the burlap.

2 Form a small ball of roving in your hands.

3 Place the ball onto the brush-style needle-felting pad and use a pen-style felting needle to felt the roving into a circle. While you are felting the roving, make sure to flip the circle over to felt both sides evenly.

4 To keep the shape of the circle, felt the sides of the roving, too. Felt until the circle is approximately 1" (3cm) in diameter.

5 Attach the felted circle to the lace using fabric adhesive. Layer two buttons and use a needle and embroidery floss to sew them together through the holes in the buttons. Using hot glue, attach the stacked buttons to the felted circle.

6 With a Crop-A-Dile, punch two holes in the square, one in each of the two upper corners. Punch a third hole in the bottom center. Set eyelets in each of the holes, using the Crop-A-Dile.

Tip

To cut burlap straight with the weave, first pull a thread out of the weave. Then cut between the threads in the gap left by the removed thread.

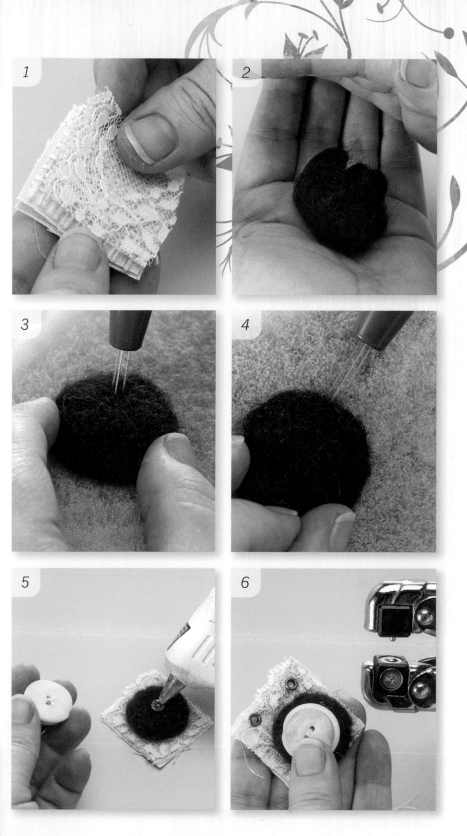

To finish this project, attach a length of pearl bead chain to each eyelet using jump rings. For some added bling, attach a chandelier bead to the end of the chain that hangs from the bottom eyelet.

Monochromatic Background

Creating a monochromatic canvas is a great way to use your trim and lace remnants.
The color of the leftovers doesn't matter because you'll be painting over each piece with
gesso and paint. All you need to do is attach the trims and textile items in a collage-like
manner to your canvas. Once the fabric adhesive dries, you can attach buttons, beads or
pearls and coat the entire canvas with several layers of gesso. Or use one coat of gesso
and the paint color of your choice. This piece is perfect to display on an easel or place in
a framed shadow box.

What You'll Need

5" × 7" (13cm × 18cm) canvas, fabric flower,
crocheted doilies, fabric trim, lace trim, buttons,
beads, fabric adhesive, gesso, paintbrush

1 Attach lace trim, fabric flowers and doilies of any color to the canvas using fabric adhesive.

2 Accent the flowers and doilies using buttons and beads.

3 Once the adhesive is dry, use a paintbrush to apply gesso directly on top of the textiles. Let dry.

4 Continue applying gesso until the colors from the textiles no longer show. Allow the gesso to dry in between coats. If you want to speed the drying process, use a heat tool.

Tip

A monochromatic background can be any color. No matter what color you choose, I suggest you paint the first layer with gesso. This will provide a good base for whatever color you choose to paint with.

To finish this project, print words on ordinary computer paper or use a rubber stamp and ink. Iron the paper between two pieces of wax paper. Cut out the words or phrases and adhere them to the piece, as desired. For a little added dimension, paint a bead of gesso around the edge of each word.

Dahlia From Quilt Scraps

This quilted dahlia is the perfect example of creating with tattered and torn textiles. Mom gave me this tattered quilt made by my great-great-aunts who lived in the old homestead in Buckhannon, West Virginia. As I thought about what I wanted to create, a tattered dahlia came to mind, as it is an old-fashioned flower that one of my aunts might have grown in her garden. The center of the dahlia is created from a vintage earring. Large earrings like this are perfect to use for flower centers; just remove the clip on the back with a few twists of a pair of pliers.

What You'll Need

Quilt scraps, large earring, cardboard, fabric adhesive, hot glue sticks, hot glue gun, 1¾" (4cm) circle punch, scissors, patterns on page 118

1 Using the patterns provided, cut fifteen of the 1½" (4cm) petals, thirteen of the 1¼" (3.2cm) petals and nine of the 1" (3cm) petals from the quilt. Fold the petals so the right and left straight edges meet, and glue them in place with hot glue. Repeat this step until all the petals have been formed.

2 Punch a 1¾" (4cm) circle from cardboard, and attach the fifteen larger petals all around the circle, seam side up.

3 Attach the medium petals on top of the large petals and slightly more toward the center of the circle.

4 Repeat step 3 using the small petals, again placing them more toward the center of the circle.

5 Once all the petals are attached, use fabric adhesive to attach a vintage-style earring for the dahlia's center.

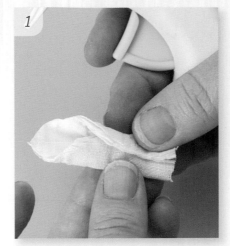
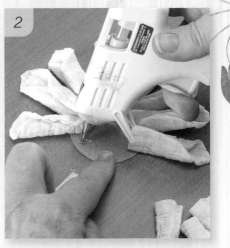

To finish this project, use fabric adhesive to attach the dahlia to a 5" × 5" (13cm × 13cm) canvas that has been wrapped with fabric.

Printed Muslin

Not all photos and collages have to be placed on a canvas. Since so much of life happens in the kitchen, using a vintage plate as the base of this collage made perfect sense. This piece features a photo of my grandfather Spinney and his siblings standing in front of the family car. To add an interesting texture to a collage like this, thread embroidery floss through each button and secure it with a double knot on the front of the button. Trim the embroidery floss and give the ends a twist with your fingers. This gives the floss a distressed look and adds dimension to the buttons.

What You'll Need

Computer paper, black-and-white photograph, muslin, clear tape, thread, pinking shears, laser printer, sewing machine

1 Using a laser printer, print a black-and-white photo onto computer paper. Place a piece of natural muslin on top of the printed photo, leaving at least a ½" (13mm) border of muslin all around the photo.

2 Using clear tape, secure the muslin edges to the paper.

3 Place the paper into your printer and print as usual. Remove the printed muslin from the paper.

4 Using a sewing machine and black thread, sew a straight stitch a few times around the edges of the photo. Using pinking shears, trim the edges of the muslin, making sure you do not cut the sewn areas.

To finish this project, cut a piece of patterned paper to fit the interior of your plate, and ink the edges of the paper. Glue the paper in place. Add your message to the rim of the plate with alphabet and number stickers. To the paper, adhere various items of your choice, including a linen heart embellishment, a piece of burlap and some lace. Adhere the printed muslin.

Add more embellishments, including crocheted doilies, threaded vintage buttons, an old earring, seam binding and paper flowers.

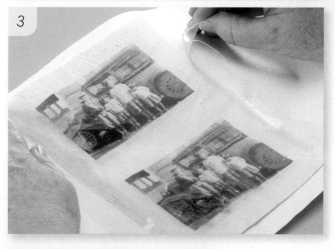

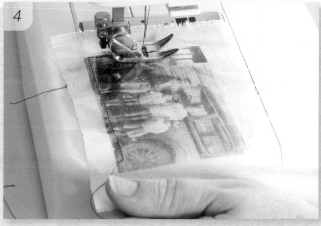

Fabric Yo-Yos

If you have only a small amount of fabric from a treasured family heirloom—such as a simple dishcloth, scarf, dress or hankie—fabric yo-yos are a perfect way to create a piece of heirloom art to pass down from generation to generation. Fabric yo-yos are beautiful when clustered together, as in this piece, or you can place one or just a few yo-yos into a fabric-lined shadow box frame with a word or name stamped onto a piece of metal. In my piece, I stamped *family*.

What You'll Need

Fabric scraps, buttons, fabric adhesive, yo-yo maker, embroidery floss, sewing needle, scissors

1 Trim your fabric remnants, vintage dish towels, hankies or feed sacks to the size required for your yo-yo maker. Place the fabric in the yo-yo maker, and position the fabric so there's an equal amount overhanging on all sides at the back of the yo-yo maker.

2 Thread the sewing needle with two strands of embroidery floss and begin stitching your yo-yo.

3 Once you have completed stitching, remove the fabric from the the yo-yo maker.

4 Pull the ends of the embroidery floss together to form the yo-yo, and tie the ends of the floss with a double knot.

5 Attach a button to the center using fabric adhesive.

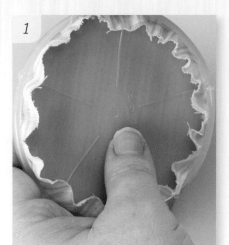

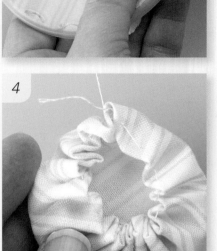

Tip

Add some variety to the piece by using some buttons with embroidery floss double knotted in the front, some with embroidery floss or thread knotted in the back and some with no thread at all. This variation keeps the textile piece from looking too uniform and predictable.

To finish the project, make a total of twenty yo-yos and layer them onto a 5" × 7" (13cm × 18cm) canvas using a fabric adhesive. Make sure each one overlaps the next just a bit.

Wrap a 7" × 9" (18cm × 23cm) canvas with a fabric remnant and secure it using fabric adhesive. Adhere a piece of lace in the center of the fabric-covered canvas. Adhere the yo-yo-covered canvas on top of that. Add a charm to one of the buttons if you'd like. To learn how to stamp a word onto the metal charm, see *Stamped Metal*, pages 56–59.

Pattern Tissue Doll

I love when one thing leads to another and then another. That's just what happened with this doll. I was getting ready to create a mini canvas when I noticed the bottle cap above the canvas and thought, *Hmmm, this looks like a head and body.* Before I knew it, the ideas started flowing, and I was on a mission to create a funky doll using all kinds of items from around my studio. It really is true that you never know when inspiration is going to hit. I had not even thought about making a doll, but because those two items came together, I was fashioning a doll from all kinds of odds and ends.

What You'll Need

3" × 3" (8cm × 8cm) canvas, sewing pattern tissue, paper trimmer or scissors, embroidery floss, fabric trim, strong liquid adhesive, fabric adhesive, seam binding, sewing needle, pinking shears

1 Fold a piece of sewing pattern tissue. Trim the tissue to 12" (30cm).

2 Then trim to 3" (8cm) wide. Leave the fold of the tissue paper intact to make stitching easier.

3 Thread a sewing needle with two strands of embroidery floss and cut the floss to 12" (30cm). Knot the end. Start a basting stitch at the top, folded edge of the paper, then sew the entire length of the tissue. While you are stitching, slightly gather the sewing pattern tissue. When finished, remove the needle.

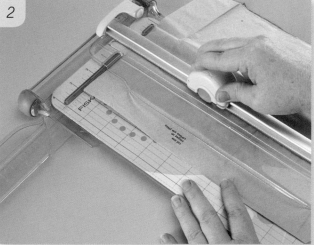

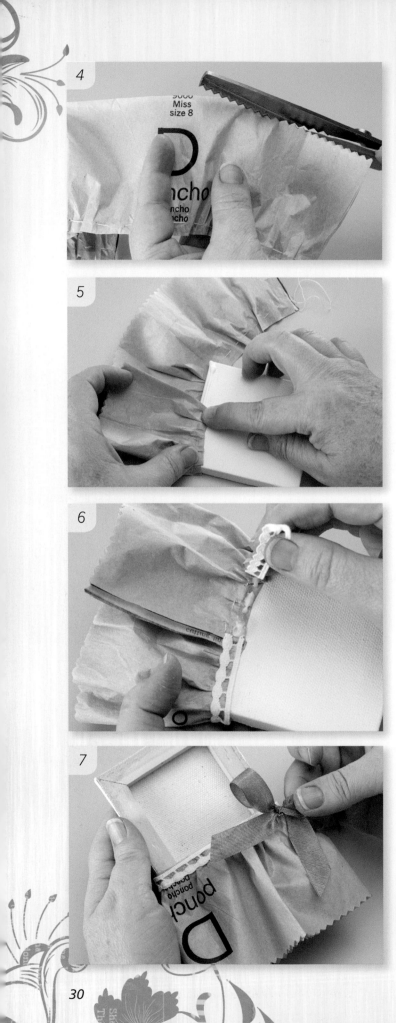

4 Use pinking shears or decorative scissors to trim the bottom edge of the skirt.

5 Gather the tissue around the 3" × 3" (8cm × 8cm) canvas so it wraps completely around the canvas. Match up the ends of the tissue at the front center of the canvas, which is the back of this project. Glue in place with strong liquid adhesive.

6 Using fabric adhesive, attach a piece of trim along the top of the sewing pattern tissue to hide the stitching on the tissue. Start where the ends of the tissue paper meet and wrap the trim around the canvas until the ends meet.

7 Create a small bow out of seam binding and attach it to the front of the piece where the trim and canvas frame meet.

To finish this project, cover the frame of the canvas with patterned paper and distress the edges with ink.

Attach two screw eyes to the bottom of the canvas, under the skirt. Make legs for the doll by wrapping paper clay around wire and leaving the wire exposed at both ends. Allow the clay to dry, then paint it. Bend the wire at the end of each leg to form a loop. From the bottom loops, hang a chandelier bead. Attach the legs to the canvas by attaching jump rings to the loops at the top of the legs, then attaching the jump rings to the screw eyes.

Attach a screw eye to the left and right side of the canvas for the arms. Cut two pieces of wire and make a loop at one end of each. String beads onto the wires. Create a loop at the end of one wire, but before closing the loop, place the loop through one of the screw eyes. Close the loop tightly. Repeat for the other beaded wire.

Transfer an image onto a button (see *To create a decal transfer* sidebar, page 85 for instructions). Use a paper piercer to open the button holes, thread embroidery floss through the button, and knot the floss. Adhere the button to the flower charm. Attach jump rings to each of the holes in the flower charm, then attach the jump rings to the ends of the beaded arms.

Cover the wing shapes with metal foil tape and adhere them to the back of the canvas.

Attach a screw eye to the top center edge of the canvas. Attach another screw eye to the bottom edge of a wooden disc. Adhere a purchased bottle cap to the wooden disc and glue a milk cap inside the bottle cap. Tie the two screw eyes together with a piece of muslin.

Fill the center opening of canvas with buttons and glue them in place. Add a chipboard heart. Stamp a word on a piece of paper, cut out the word, and ink the edges. Adhere the word to the canvas.

Fabric Wrapped Mobile

When I have an idea without a theme, I simply start pulling things together that I like and think will work together. I knew I wanted to create a mobile from the lamp shade I found at a thrift store. As I attached various found objects, the piece began to remind me of all the tea parties I had as a child with my grandmother Spinney. Grammy was the queen of tea parties. So I attached a frame with a photo of her and me together and another frame with few dried pansies. Even though I had no theme, I trusted in my creative thoughts and ended up with a treasured memory mobile.

What You'll Need

Metal frame lamp shade with outer covering removed, fabric, fabric adhesive, scissors

1 Make a small cut in your fabric about 1" (3cm) from the edge.

2 Holding the fabric on each side of the cut, rip the fabric into a strip.

3 Apply a small amount of fabric adhesive on one end of the fabric strip and begin wrapping the fabric strip around the metal frame of the lamp shade.

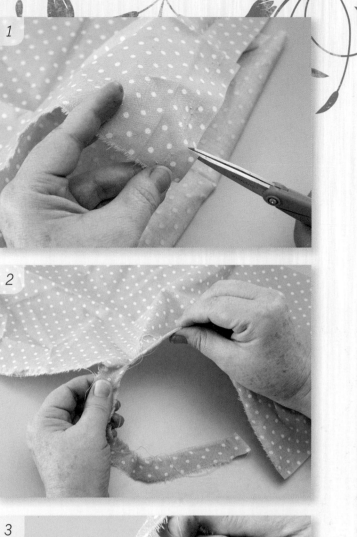

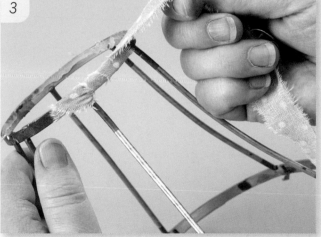

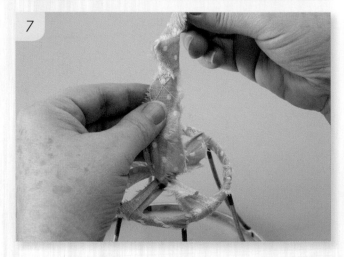

4 Continue wrapping until you are back to where you started. Trim any excess fabric. Secure the fabric strip by applying a small amount of fabric adhesive on the end of the strip and holding it in place.

5 At the top of the lamp shade, place a strip of fabric under the frame at the nine o'clock and three o'clock positions. Double knot the fabric strip at the top center of the lamp shade. Be sure to catch both layers of fabric as you tie the second knot. Trim the ends of the fabric.

6 Repeat step 5 with fabric placed at the twelve and six o'clock positions. The two fabric strips attached at the top of the metal frame form an **X**.

7 To create a hanger for your mobile, tie a fabric strip to the center knot on top of the lamp shade. Tie the fabric in a double knot. Then tie a knot at the end with the two loose ends of the fabric.

Continue cutting the fabric strips and wrapping them tightly until the entire frame is wrapped.

Rip five fabric strips and trim them to different lengths; all should be long enough to hang below the bottom edge of the lamp shade. Tie a fabric strip to each fabric bridge created when you tied the **X** to the top of the lamp shade, and tie one to the center of the **X**.

Making Candy Mold Charms

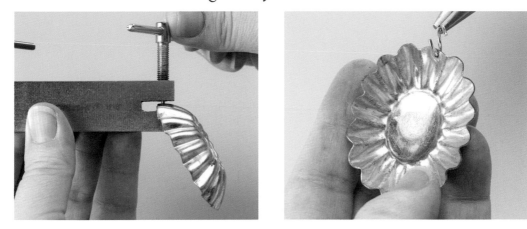

1. Place the center end of a candy mold into a two-hole punch.
2. Slowly screw the handle of the punch until a hole has been created. Unscrew the handle of the punch and remove the candy mold. Using pliers, attach a jump ring through the hole.

To finish this project, tie as many as three charms or other items to each fabric strip. These items may include metal frames filled with an image or dried flowers, keys, candy molds with holes drilled into them or a small perfume bottle.

Thread embroidery floss into the holes of three buttons and tie a knot at the front of each. Adhere each button to the center of a lace flower, then adhere the flowers to the outside of the lamp shade frame. (I cut my lace flowers from vintage doilies.)

Loop pearl bead chain onto the bottom of the lamp shade frame, and attach chandelier beads to each vertical spine of the frame.

Chapter Two
Metal

In this chapter, you will learn how to incorporate all things metal into your projects. When thrifting, I'm always looking for interesting metal items I can use in my projects. Some of the pieces I keep my eyes open for are gelatin molds and tart tins; stainless steel spoons, forks and butter knives; small medicine tins; thimbles and keys. These are easy to find, and you can usually get them at a great price. But metal foil tape and copper sheeting are also great products to use in projects. I will show you how to create a pretty accent from a vintage thimble, and you'll make a unique family tree with photo transfers on hammered metal spoons. Each project incorporates metal elements in fascinating ways. I'm certain you will look at these items in an entirely new light.

Wire Skirt

Working with the bits and pieces I've found over the years really stirs my imagination. All of the items for this project are treasures I found while digging in thrift shops and flea markets. The idea for the doll came while I was putting away the gelatin molds. I noticed the two similar molds stacked on top of each other resembled a skirt. Inspiration struck, and before I knew it, I was digging in my stash of vintage items. Her eclectic look is just what I wanted, and she sits proudly in my studio.

What You'll Need

24-gauge wire, seam binding, beads, buttons, embroidery floss, wire cutters, needle-nose pliers

1 Using wire cutters, cut four pieces of 24-gauge wire to 12" (30cm), one piece to 11" (28cm), one piece to 14" (36cm) and one piece to 16" (41cm). Cross two of the 12" (30cm) wire pieces to form an **X** and twist the middle to secure.

2 Create a second **X** with the two remaining 12" (30cm) pieces. Place this **X** on top of the first, offset slightly, and twist to secure them.

3 Bend the wires down to form a dome.

4 Take the 11" (28cm) wire and start wrapping it around the dome about one-third of the way down from the top. Wrap the wire around each of the wires that creates the frame of the dome.

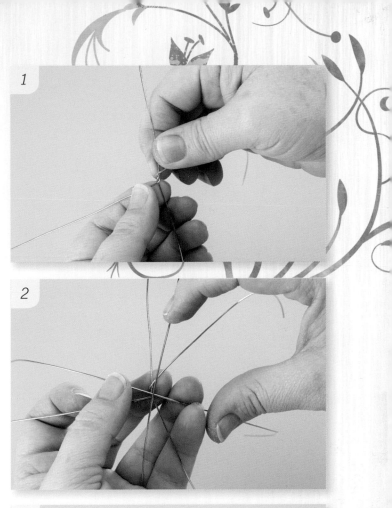

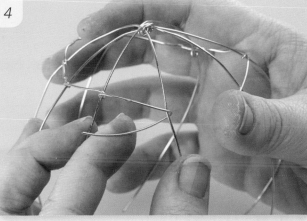

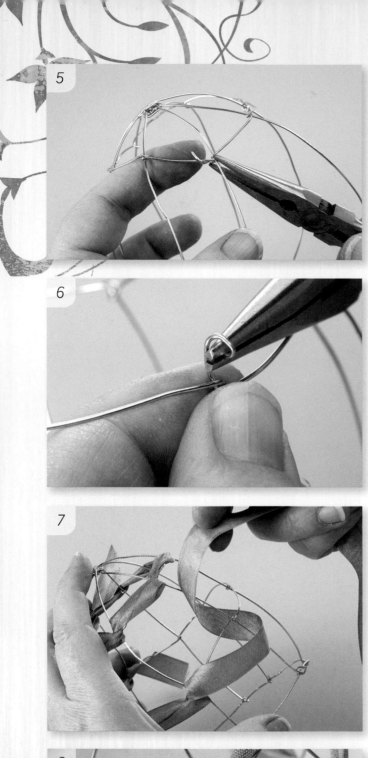

5 When you get to the end of the wire, twist the end around one of the framework wires and use pliers to secure the end in place.

6 Repeat with the remaining pieces of wire; wrap the 14" (36cm) piece around the middle of the skirt and the 16" (41cm) piece around the bottom. Then use the needle-nose pliers to form decorative loops at the ends of the framework wires.

7 Loop seam binding around the top, middle and bottom horizontal wires. Be sure to cover the areas where the wires intertwine.

8 Accent the wire with beads and buttons. These beads came off old earrings, but you can use any kind of beads. Attach them with headpins or loops of wire.

9 Tie buttons to the bottom wire with embroidery floss.

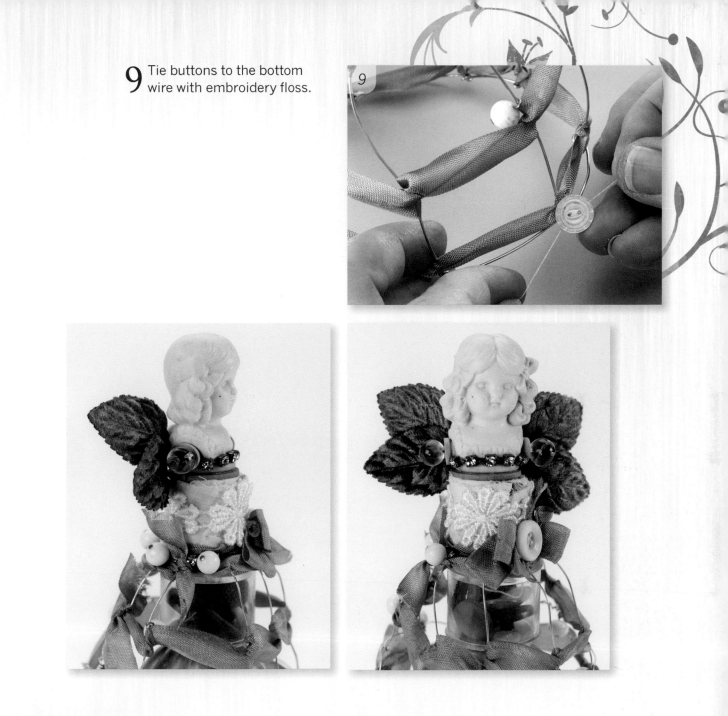

To finish this project, glue two vintage gelatin molds together to form the interior of the skirt. Adhere a small plastic cylinder (such as a bottle top or vintage zipper holder) filled with buttons to the molds. Slip the wire skirt over this and affix with strong liquid adhesive.

Wrap a large wooden spool with fabric and then with lace, and use fabric adhesive to secure them. Glue the spool to the top of the skirt.

Cut a piece of wire and make a loop in one end. Slide a bead onto the wire. Place the wire through a small wooden spool. Slide a second bead onto the wire and create another loop to secure it. Attach the doll head to this spool and affix to the top of the large spool. Decorate the doll with rhinestones. Arrange four fabric leaves to look like wings and glue them to the back of the doll.

Faux Gold

This is a tribute to my great-grandfather and great-grandmother Rand. The photo was taken on their wedding day. I wanted this vintage cigarette tin to resemble a keepsake found hidden in a chest or drawer that holds mementos from their special day. I added a faux gold finish to the edges of the frame around the photo and lace and doilies that may have been found on a wedding dress. The rhinestone trim and button represent her wedding dress or earrings. The vintage buttons are for my great-grandfather's shirt, and the black seam binding bow is in honor of his suit. When all these finds are put together, I think it truly represents their wedding day.

What You'll Need

Metal tin, embossing ink, embossing powder, heat tool, clothespin

42

1 Apply embossing ink to one outer edge of a small metal tin.

2 Sprinkle gold embossing powder on top of the embossing ink.

3 Using a heat tool, heat the embossing powder until it melts. Continue these steps on all four sides of the metal tin until it is completely covered with gold embossing powder. The tin may get hot so use a clothespin to hold it, if you'd like.

Reapply embossing ink and gold embossing powder to areas of the metal tin that might not be completely covered, if needed, and heat with a heat tool.

To finish this project, trim the laser-printed photo to fit the inside of the metal tin. Back the photo with cardboard to make it sturdier, and adhere it to the tin with an adhesive foam dot. To age the photo, you can apply beeswax to the image before placing it in the tin. To learn how to cover a photo with beeswax, see *Objects Embedded in Beeswax*, pages 66–69.

Cut patterned paper to fit into the cigarette tin. To the left side, glue a piece of lace to the patterned paper. Layer more lace and a string of pearls to the left side.

To add glitter to the chipboard letters, paint the letters in a color close to that of the glitter you are using. In my case, I painted the letters with silver metallic acrylic paint. Apply dimensional adhesive to the top of each letter. Generously apply silver glass glitter to the adhesive until the adhesive is completely covered. Let the glitter settle into the adhesive. Holding the letter with tweezers, gently tap off the excess glitter. Set aside to dry, then adhere them to the page.

To the right side, adhere the small tin. Glue lace around the tin. Add two rhinestone chains to the page, partially outlining the small tin with one of them. Tie buttons to the lace with embroidery floss. Adhere a Frozen Charlotte doll (see *Molded Embellishments*, pages 72–73), brooch, seam binding and earring to the lace.

Faux Tintype

My mom has a framed tintype of my great-great-grandmother Rebecca Hinkle. I have always loved this photo and thought I would try creating my own faux tintype. You can imagine how thrilled I was to discover my idea actually worked. The copper sheeting peeking out from the black acrylic paint accents the black-and-white photo of Rebecca perfectly.

What You'll Need

Copper sheeting, computer paper, image and sentiment printed with a laser printer, black acrylic paint, matte medium, paper towel, paintbrush, craft knife, cutting mat, scissors, embossing folder, embossing machine

Tip

To distress the copper even more, lightly rub a small piece of steel wool over the copper areas where the paint has been wiped off.

1 Carefully cut a piece of copper sheeting and computer paper large enough to cover the inside of your embossing folder.

2 Place the sheeting and paper in the folder and follow the instructions for your embossing machine. If there is excess sheeting, trim the edges while it's still in the folder to ensure your lines are straight and to help prevent cutting yourself with the sharp copper. Remove the embossed sheeting and paper.

3 Set the paper aside. Using a paintbrush, apply black acrylic paint to the front of the copper piece, making sure to get paint into all the grooves.

4 Use a damp paper towel to wipe off the excess paint.

5 Place the embossed paper on a cutting mat, and using your craft knife, cut out the center oval shape and the area above the oval where the name or title will go. This is your template for cutting your photo and title. Place the template over the photo. Using a pencil, lightly trace around the inside edge of the oval.

6 With scissors, cut out the photo, then attach it to the faux tintype using matte medium. Repeat steps 5 and 6 for the title.

To finish this project, paint a 5" × 7" (13cm × 18cm) gallery-wrapped canvas with black acrylic paint, and when dry, highlight the edges with gold paint. Cover the patterned paper with crackle paint, and when dry, apply ink over the cracks to accentuate them. Adhere the paper to the top of the canvas. Adhere the tintype to the canvas using adhesive foam dots so it is raised just a bit.

Metal stamp a word onto a piece of copper tape, following the steps for *Stamped Metal*, pages 56–59. Adhere the label to the paper below the tintype.

Riveted Patchwork

This patchwork heart represents all the layers of love I've received from and have for my family and friends; each layer is secured tightly and cherished. Not wanting to distract from the heart embellishment, I kept the background rather simple and decided vintage sheet music would work beautifully. To accent the rivets in the altered heart, I designed a scalloped border from metal foil sheets. This is another great way to use your border punches.

What You'll Need

Metal foil tape sheets, chipboard heart, paper towel, acrylic paint, alcohol ink, felt pad and blending tool, steel wool, paintbrush, ballpoint pen, scissors

Tip

Remove the excess metal foil tape from inside the scallop border punch after each use. If you don't, it might get bunched up inside the punch.

1 Using scissors, cut metal foil tape into random shapes and sizes. Remove the backing from the tape and adhere to the chipboard heart, overlapping the pieces.

2 Burnish the edges of the heart and trim the excess foil.

3 Using a click-style ballpoint pen with the tip retracted, press the pen opening firmly onto the foil along the seam lines. The indentation from the pen looks like the outer circle of a rivet. While the pen is still in place, press the top of the pen down, as if to write with the pen, to create the center circle of the rivet.

4 After you have all the rivets you need, use a paintbrush to apply a thin layer of acrylic paint on top of the heart. Use a damp paper towel to gently wipe away the excess paint.

5 Apply alcohol ink onto the felt pad of a blending tool and randomly apply it over the heart.

6 Using a piece of steel wool, burnish the surface to remove some of the ink and distress the heart.

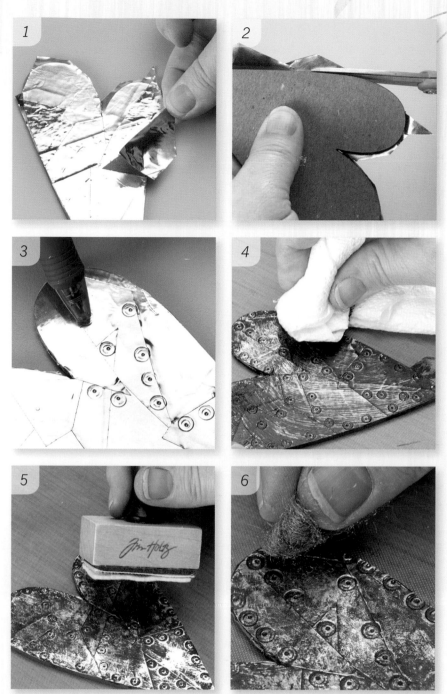

To finish this piece, adhere patterned paper to the top of a 5" × 5" (13cm × 13cm) gallery-wrapped canvas. Brush the surface with clear crackle paint, and distress with ink when dry.

Cut four pieces of metal foil tape to fit each side of your canvas. Use a scallop border punch to cut a scallop border from the tape. Continue until the length of the foil has been punched. Repeat for the remaining pieces of tape.

Attach the scallop borders to the edges of the canvas. Accent in between each punched hole in the border by pressing the end of a stylus into the foil tape to create a small dot. Using a black gel pen, fill in each of the punched holes and outline the scalloped edges. Mount the riveted heart to the center of the canvas with adhesive foam dots.

Faux Mercury Glass

I'm not sure why it is, but I love to open little boxes and tins that I find when thrifting and antiquing. In them, I've found long-lost treasures. So making this little shadow box album made me think of all the treasures I've found. I wanted this one to resemble a keepsake from long ago, so I included items that could have been of meaning to a girl in the past. The faux mercury glass in each square is something you will want to create over and over again. You can use this technique on any type of clear glass (thrift store vases, candlesticks and more).

What You'll Need

Clear glass, mist bottle, Looking Glass mirror spray paint, paper towel

1 Fill a mist bottle with water and lightly mist the clear glass.

2 Spray a layer of mirror spray paint onto the glass, on top of the water. Let the spray paint dry for several minutes.

3 Using a paper towel, wipe the glass to remove the water droplets. The more water droplets on the glass, the more clear areas you will have. Less water will give you a more mirrored effect. Experiment on a scrap of clear glass to determine the look you like best.

Tip

You can repeat the technique for more than one application, depending on the amount of mirror finish you want.

To finish this piece, collage the back (with the exposed frames) and sides of two mini canvases with patterned paper and gesso so they resemble picture frames. Place a piece of quilt, wrong side up, on a table, and glue the canvases side by side with a small space between them. The quilt fabric acts as the cover of the book. If you sandwich ribbon between the quilt and the canvases, the ribbon will serve as a tie closure. You can also embellish the outside of the book, adding a crocheted doily and a vintage button.

On the left inside of the book, stamp or cut out an image of your choice. Ink the edges of the image, insert it into the opening and add the mercury glass over the image. Secure in place with a bead of clear-drying glue around all edges.

On the right, insert the mercury glass directly into the opening and secure with a bead of clear-drying glue. With fabric glue or hot glue, add embellishments such as a crocheted doily, a heart covered with patterned paper, an earring, paper flowers and a small bottle filled with beads and tied with baker's twine.

Decorate the edges of the frame, as desired. I drew small scalloped shapes with a charcoal pencil. To prevent the charcoal pencil from smearing, spray it with protective sealer. I did not seal mine, as I like the smudged and smeared look.

Soda Can Flowers

I really enjoyed creating the background for these soda can flowers. I used the wallpaper pieces that I had pulled off the walls of the old homestead in Buckhannon, West Virginia. I think the combination of the transfer decals, charcoal pencil and white polka dots creates a beautiful collage background that perfectly complements the color and texture of these soda can flowers.

What You'll Need

Two empty aluminum cans, rhinestone buttons or beads, acrylic paint, ink, strong adhesive tape, hot glue sticks, hot glue gun, paintbrush, sandpaper, blending tool (optional), tin snips, die cut machine, flower die (3D Wrapped Flower by Sizzix), polka-dot embossing folder

1 Using tin snips, carefully cut the top and bottom off of two aluminum cans.

2 Cut down one side of each can so you can make the metal pieces flat.

3 Place the metal onto the flower die and cut it according to your cutting machine's instructions. Repeat until you have the number of die cuts needed to create each flower: You will need two large wrapped flowers and one small wrapped flower to create the larger flower; two small wrapped flowers to create the medium-size flower; and one small wrapped flower to create the smallest flower. Place the cut flower pieces into a polka-dot embossing folder and emboss per your embossing machine's instructions.

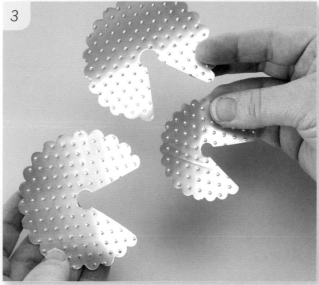

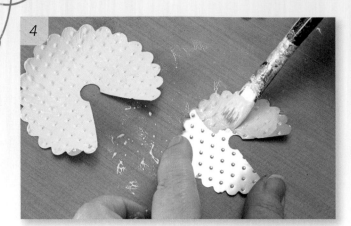

4 Apply acrylic paint to the unprinted side of each wrapped flower with a paintbrush.

5 Once the paint is dry, use sandpaper to distress the petals.

6 Using the tin snips, cut in between each scallop about two-thirds of the way down on each die cut. Do not cut all the way through or your flower will fall apart.

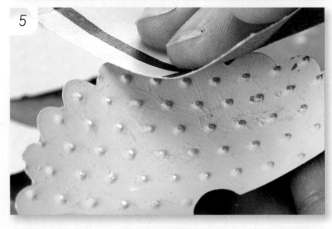

7 On the large wrapped flower, apply a piece of strong adhesive tape to the top of one end petal at the very end of the petal. Place the petal from the opposite end on top of the tape, and press down firmly to secure in place. Repeat this step to join all the flowers.

8 Carefully bend and shape the petals so they look like natural flowers and are no longer uniform. At the same time, dab the flowers with ink for added color and texture, using a blending tool, if desired.

9 Using a hot glue gun, place a small dot of glue in the center of one of the large joined flowers. Place the second large joined flower on top of the hot glue and allow the glue to cool in place.

10 Place a dot of hot glue in the center of the second joined flower and place a small joined flower on top of the hot glue. Allow the glue to cool in place. Accent the center of the flower with a rhinestone button attached with hot glue.

11 Continue these same steps to create the smaller flowers. For the medium-sized flower, layer two small joined flowers. For the small flower, you need only one of the wrapped flowers. Attach rhinestone buttons or beads to the center of each flower.

Tip

To give a vintage, aged look to your projects, apply a water-based ink like Distress Ink by Ranger. Use a damp cloth or paper towel to gently wipe away some of the ink. Non-water-based inks dry too quickly to wipe away and become permanent.

To finish this project, paint a 4" × 4" (10cm × 10cm) gallery-wrapped canvas a cream color. When dry, adhere the collage elements including wallpaper pieces and patterned paper. Use a paintbrush and matte medium to adhere the papers to the canvas. When dry, accent a few areas with transfer decals (see *To create a decal transfer* sidebar, page 85, for this technique). Highlight the edges of the canvas with white paint polka dots and hand-drawn scallops with charcoal pencil. Adhere the flowers to the canvas with hot glue.

Assemblage Necklace

Taking bits and pieces of broken jewelry and combining them is such a fun and simple way to create new unique jewelry pieces. You will find all kinds of items mixed and matched in this necklace: pearl bead chain, chandelier beads, a vintage button, even a butter knife. Simply attach the bits and pieces until you achieve the desired length for your necklace. My necklace is approximately 20" (51 cm) long, as I like to put it on by simply putting it over my head. But you can add a clasp to yours, if you prefer.

What You'll Need

Butter knife, pearl bead chain, pearl bead chain with crystals, chandelier bead, self-adhesive pearls, two jump rings, 20-gauge wire, rhinestone button with shank, tweezers, hacksaw, jewelry pliers, wire cutters, drill

1 Using a hacksaw, saw a vintage butter knife in two pieces: the handle and the blade. Using a drill with a drill bit large enough for the wire to fit through, drill a small hole in the top of the handle. Save the blade for another use, such as making a *Stamped Metal* embellishment (see pages 56-59).

2 Attach a small strand of pearl bead chain to a crystal chandelier bead. Attach 20-gauge wire to one end of the strand of beads and run the wire up inside the knife handle and through the hole.

3 Attach a small strand of beads to the end of the wire, and wrap the wire to secure it in place.

4 Attach two jump rings to the shank of a rhinestone button using a pair of pliers. Attach a small strand of pearl bead chain and chandelier beads to each jump ring using a pair of pliers. Attach a mixture of pearl bead chain and pearl bead chain with crystals to the end of each strand of beads using a pair of pliers. The length of the chain is up to you, as this determines the length of the necklace.

5 Accent the knife front with self-adhesive pearls.

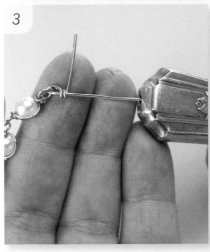

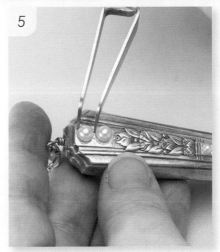

Stamped Metal

Personalizing projects with metal-stamped charms or embellishments is a simple way to create unique pieces. Metal stamping does require a few basic supplies. I highly recommend you purchase a brass head metal-stamping hammer, a steel stamping block and Stamp Straight Tape. These tools will make your stamping so much easier and much more successful. Believe me—I've stamped with an old hammer and ended up getting double-stamped images; I've been on my knees using the garage floor as a stamping block; and I metal stamped more crooked pieces than I care to admit.

What You'll Need

Metal charm, acrylic paint or permanent marker, paper towel or steel wool, thick tape (like Stamp Straight Tape), metal stamps, brass hammer, bench block

1 Place your charm onto the bench block. Apply the tape along the area you want the stamped letter to be placed. In this case, you are stamping vertically, so place the tape horizontally in the center of the charm. The tape is your guide to keep your letters straight. For added precision, you can use a pencil to mark the charm where you want each letter to be stamped. Just remember, this is handmade and won't be perfect no matter how hard you try, so embrace the imperfection.

2 Starting with the middle letter of your word, place the metal stamp on the charm. Make sure the bottom edge of the letter lines up with the top edge of the tape. Hold the stamp so it is flat on the charm, and strike the stamp with medium to firm pressure. If the stamp has not moved, you can strike it again; if the stamp has moved, you do take a chance of getting a double strike mark.

3 Remove the tape and move the charm on the bench block to stamp the next letter. Realign the tape on the charm for each letter you stamp. Repeat until you have stamped the entire word.

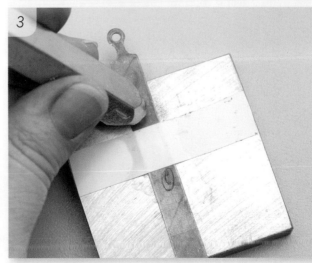

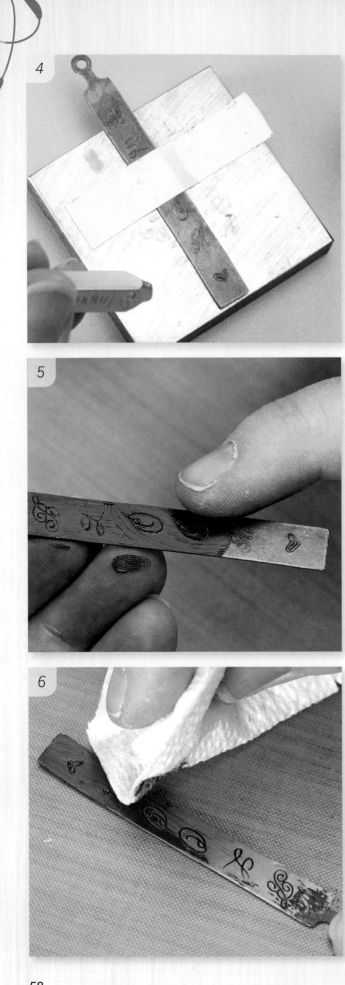

4 Stamp a small metal heart at the base of the word.

5 Apply black acrylic paint or permanent marker to the letters on the charm.

6 With a damp paper towel or steel wool (for a more distressed look), rub the excess paint from around each letter.

To finish this piece, create a 7" × 9" (18cm × 23cm) collage of sewn papers, following the technique on page 109. Stamp words onto the collage with black archival ink, if desired. Adhere the collage to a 7" × 9" (18cm × 23cm) canvas.

To create the floral centerpiece, glue two tart tins or similar pieces of metal together and embellish them with a milk bottle top for the center. Adhere the flower to the canvas with strong liquid adhesive.

Adhere patterned paper to the front of the bottle and around the neck.

Starting at the cut end of the wire, fashion a free-form leaf, looping the cut end of the wire around the wire on the spool to secure it in place. Unroll more wire to create the stem, then cut the wire. Wrap the wire with muslin strips, following the technique featured in *Fabric Wrapped Mobile*, pages 32–35. Insert the wire into the neck of the bottle and secure it with strong liquid adhesive, if necessary.

Tie the stamped charm and a few beads and button to a piece of baker's twine, and tie the twine around the neck of the bottle. Adhere the bottle to the canvas and tuck the stem under the flower head.

Thimble Charm

Mini canvases are perfect for creating mini shadow boxes. I love soldering, but by no means do I feel comfortable in instructing you how to solder. The next best thing to use is metal foil tape. One advantage of using metal tape is that you can cut all kinds of different edges using decorative scissors. The real star here, though, is the vintage thimble charm. Be sure to really make it your own by adding bits that are meaningful to you. I, of course, have added glass glitter, rhinestones and pearls along with a bit of vintage-style printing and ribbon.

What You'll Need

Metal thimble, glass vial with cork stopper, glass glitter, screw eye, rhinestone trim, pearl bead chain, butterfly charm, muslin scrap, seam binding, word printed on paper, 16-gauge wire, strong liquid adhesive, clear-drying adhesive, ink, wire cutters, needle-nose pliers, drill

1 Drill a hole that is large enough for the wire to pass through into the top of a metal thimble.

2 Fill a small glass bottle with glass glitter. Screw a screw eye in the center of the cork, and firmly place the cork back into the bottle. Apply a thin layer of clear-drying adhesive to the edge of the cork before placing it into the bottle. Once dry, the cork will stay securely in place.

Cut a 2" (5cm) piece of 16-gauge wire. Create a loop in the wire and thread on the pearl bead chain, bottle, butterfly charm and rhinestone trim. Use pliers to squeeze the wire together to secure.

3 Thread the wire through the hole in the thimble. Using pliers, create a loop by bending the wire downward; this will be the hanger for your charm.

4 Tie a strip of muslin and seam binding to the loop at the top of the thimble. Cut the word from the piece of paper, and ink the edges using brown ink. Adhere to the smooth portion of the thimble.

To finish this project, cover the mini canvas with patterned paper. Screw a screw eye into the center bottom edge of the canvas. Working on the back of the canvas, adhere embellishments into the hole created by the canvas's frame. Include a molded doll (see *Molded Embellishments*, pages 72–73) aged with acrylic paint, a button embellished with a transfer decal (see *To create a decal transfer* sidebar, page 85), paper posies and a paper butterfly embellished with a rhinestone.

Cut the art modeling film to the size of the canvas and place over the canvas back. Secure the film to the canvas with metal foil tape. Cut a decorative edge on the tape with pinking shears before applying, if desired. Open the wire loop at the top of the thimble charm, and attach the thimble to the screw eye on the canvas. Close the wire securely.

Photo Transfer Onto Metal

The distressed images of vintage tintypes are the inspiration behind this family tree wall hanging. I thought it would be fun to create a family tree with photo transfers of my grandmother Spinney, my great-grandparents and my great-great-grandparents onto vintage aluminum tins and silver spoons that I flattened using a hammer. Since my great-grandparents owned a laundry service, I attached their photos from pearl bead chain hung from an old wooden pants hanger. The buttons are part of the laundry theme, but I attached some sparkling rhinestones to them to tie in the vial of glitter. I love this family tree wall hanging and will display it proudly in my studio.

What You'll Need

Metal tin, image printed on a laser printer, matte medium, paintbrush, mist bottle filled with water, brayer, heat tool (optional)

Tip

This same transfer technique can be used on paper tags, wood pieces, canvas and many other surfaces.

1 Cut the photo to the size of the tin back. Apply a somewhat thick layer of matte medium to the back of the tin with a paintbrush, and apply a thin layer to the photograph.

2 Place the photo face down onto the metal tin. Using a brayer, carefully roll out any bubbles. Clean off your brayer between each use. Do not get any of the matte medium onto the back of the paper; otherwise it will be hard to remove the paper once the medium has dried.

3 Allow the medium to dry. You can speed the drying process with a heat tool, if desired.

4 Once dry, mist water on the back of the photo.

5 Using your finger, gently rub off the paper. Once the paper is removed, you will see the transferred image on the tin.

6 Apply a little matte medium to the tin with your fingertip to help hide any remaining tiny pieces of paper and to seal the image.

To finish this project, adhere patterned paper to a wooden hanger. Adhere buttons to one side of the hanger, and wrap the hook with muslin following the technique featured in *Fabric Wrapped Mobile*, pages 32–35. Twist screw eyes into the bottom of the hanger, as desired.

Assemble a dangle of varying lengths for each screw eye. Mix pearl bead chain, charms, buttons and whatever else you'd like. To turn the metal tin into a dangle, drill holes in both ends of the tin and add pearl bead chain and a charm.

Flatten some metal spoons (hammering directly on the spoons for a distressed look). Use metal stamps to spell out words or messages on one side of each hammered spoon (see *Stamped Metal*, pages 56–59). Use the technique above to transfer photos to the other side of the spoon. Be sure to do the transfers after any hammering.

ADOPT
THE
PACE
OT
NATURE

Sweet
Old Love
"Song

5 · 1 · 9 · 9

Strichmaker
CANAL DOVER, O.

Chapter Three
Wax, Resin & Clay

This chapter is where we get a little bit messy—but only a bit. I have never been really big on messy. (I have a photo that proves this point: me at age one wearing a white dress with cake all over my mouth, but not one bit is on my dress or hands—and I wasn't wearing a bib!) So if you are like me, don't worry. This chapter is all about altering items with embossing powders, resin, jewelry clay, melted embossing enamel and beeswax! I'll show you how to create a mold using vintage finds so you can create duplicate pieces and save your original to display. You will create a wildflower bouquet that will stand the test of time, and you will see how easy it is to encase a pendant in resin to complement a charm bracelet filled with vintage baubles. Get ready to make some beautiful art.

Objects Embedded in Beeswax

One of my favorite vintage items is the old-fashioned Putz house. I decided to create a template for my own house and encase it in beeswax. Embedding items into melted beeswax is so fun. And the great thing is, if you don't like the item you embedded in your art, all you need to do is reheat the beeswax and carefully remove the object with a pair of tweezers. I accented the house by embedding one of my favorite photos of my great-grandmother Rand on her wedding day. It's the perfect photo for a love-themed project—"This is the house that love built."

What You'll Need

House patterns on page 118, cardboard, patterned paper, natural beeswax pellets, beeswax crayons, buttons, microbeads, images and words printed on a laser printer, feather, dried flower, rhinestone trim, strong liquid adhesive, tweezers, quilting iron, heat tool

1 Trace the house and roof patterns onto lightweight cardboard and cut out. Score along the dashed lines shown on the pattern. Apply strong liquid adhesive on the outside of the house and roof pieces. Place patterned paper on the adhesive and trim the paper to size. Form the house by folding on the scored lines. Use a bone folder to crease the folds to make them nice and crisp. Apply strong liquid adhesive to the shorter tab at the end of the house and secure in place underneath the longer tab.

Heat your quilting iron to high and then switch it to low. Place several natural beeswax pellets onto the paper. Melt the wax with the iron.

2 As the beeswax melts, drag the wax along the paper. Continue to add beeswax pellets until the entire house is covered and you have the thickness of beeswax you like. I prefer a fairly thin layer.

3 Trim your image to size, and place it onto the front of the house. Rub the iron over the top of the photo lightly to melt the beeswax underneath the photo. Place a few pellets of beeswax on top of the photo and melt them over the photo using the iron.

4 Using the same technique, emboss a dried flower into the wax and then a feather. Continue to add items, including words cut from paper, covering each with the desired thickness of beeswax.

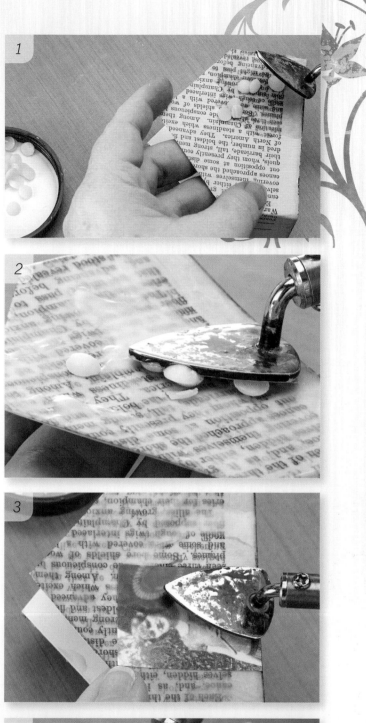

5 To attach the rhinestone trim, place the trim around the edges of the photo. Use a heat tool to gently and carefully heat the wax around the rhinestone trim.

6 While the wax is still warm, use tweezers to gently press the rhinestone trim into the wax.

7 Attach the buttons to the paper of the roof piece with a little liquid adhesive. Once the adhesive is dry, place beeswax pellets on top of the buttons and melt the wax with the iron.

8 When the beeswax is as thick as you like, swipe the hot iron over the wax to melt it slightly and sprinkle a few gold micro-beads into the hot wax to add color and texture.

Tip

If you want to speed up the process of covering the buttons, melt the beeswax in a melting pot per the manufacturer's instructions. Using a natural bristle brush, apply the melted wax to the buttons. You can smooth the wax with a heat tool or iron. (See *Molded Embellishments*, pages 72–73, for more on using a melting pot.)

9 Touch a black beeswax crayon to the hot iron, allowing the crayon to melt onto the iron.

10 Swipe the iron along the edges of the house to transfer the wax. Continue steps 9–10 until all the edges of the house and roof are accented.

To finish this project, create a base for your house. Adhere a quilt strip around a wooden spool. Embellish the spool with twine and vintage buttons, if desired. Cover a mini canvas with paper and wax, as in steps 1–3. Accent the edges with wax crayon. Glue the spool onto the back of the canvas to form a display base. Attach the house to the base using strong liquid adhesive. Adhere the roof to the house. Add embellishments, such as a seam binding bow, feathers and fabric flowers, if desired.

Wax Engraving

This photo has always been one of my favorites of me and my grandmother Spinney. I clearly remember the day this picture was taken, as it was my aunt Linda's wedding. I had briefly fallen asleep in the pew, and I woke up to the organ playing and Aunt Linda walking down the aisle. Since this canvas was inspired by love, I chose sheet music hearts to embed into the beeswax. One great thing about combining paper and beeswax is that the paper becomes a bit transparent once the melted wax is applied. In this piece, I like how the handwriting from the ledger paper shows through the photo.

What You'll Need

5" × 5" (13cm × 13cm) gallery-wrapped canvas, patterned paper, natural beeswax pellets, pearlescent powdered pigment, stylus, paintbrush, rubber stamp, stencil, paper punch, quilting iron, heat tool

1 Adhere a piece of patterned paper to the top of your canvas. Place the beeswax pellets on the paper and melt with the quilting iron. Apply several layers of wax.

2 Heat the wax slightly and embed hearts punched from patterned paper (see *Objects Embedded in Beeswax*, pages 66–69, for more on embedding).

3 Heat an area of the wax with a heat tool, then press a rubber stamp into the heated wax. Once the wax cools, lift the stamp to reveal the stamped image.

4 Using a stylus, trace around each heart to create a grooved outline.

5 To create circles, place a polka-dot stencil on top of the wax, and use a stylus to trace the inside of each circle.

6 To add color and luminosity, use a paintbrush to apply powdered pigment to the wax.

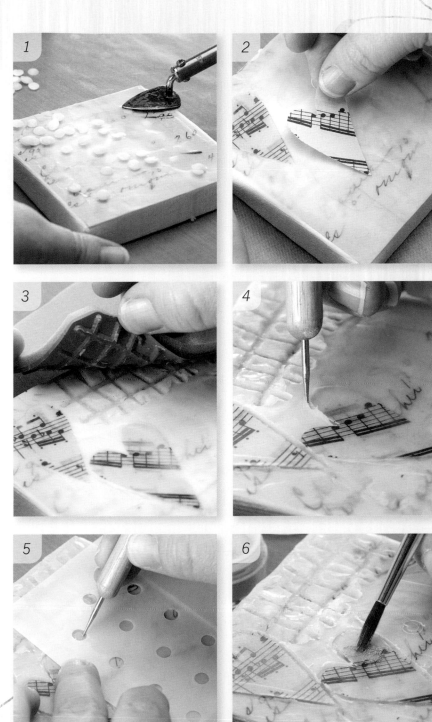

To finish this project, embed a third heart, more patterned paper, a doily and a photo. Apply a bit more wax over the top of each. Apply additional powdered pigments to the wax. Cover the sides of the canvas with patterned paper, then accent the edges by applying brown and white beeswax using the technique shown in steps 9 and 10 of *Objects Embedded in Beeswax*, pages 66–69.

Molded Embellishments

While on treasure hunts in flea markets and such, I try to purchase as many items as I can in bulk to use in workshops. Often that's just not possible, for instance when I'm buying an item I really love, like bisque doll busts and Frozen Charlotte dolls. My solution is to make a mold of the item and produce as many as I need. One benefit of working with a molded item is that it has a flat back so you can easily attach it to all kinds of altered projects.

What You'll Need

Item from which to a create mold, clear ultrathick embossing enamel (UTEE), white ultrathick embossing enamel (UTEE), two-part molding putty, nonstick craft sheet, rubber spatula, heat tool, melting pot

1 Roll two balls of equal size, one from each of the putty containers. Knead the balls together until the color becomes uniform. Form a disc that is large enough to cover the front of the item to be molded. Place the putty onto a nonstick craft sheet and press the item into it; let cure for about 10 minutes. Once the putty has cured, gently lift the item out of the mold.

2 Place the melting pot onto the nonstick craft sheet. Heat the melting pot on the UTEE setting for several minutes with the lid in place. Pour in the clear UTEE to the max line and add a few sprinkles of white UTEE. The white UTEE is concentrated, so you do not need to use much. Replace the lid and allow the enamel to melt.

Use the spatula to gently mix the white with the clear. If you mix too vigorously, you will create bubbles. If this happens, use your heat tool to pop the bubbles by applying a little heat to the surface of the melted UTEE.

3 Carefully pour the UTEE into the mold. Let it set for a few minutes.

4 Once it has set, remove the embellishment from the mold.

To finish this project, punch holes in the top corners of a cardboard frame. Insert a piece of seam binding for the hanger, and tie it in place. Embellish one end of the seam binding with buttons and twine.

Cover the photo opening with patterned paper. Embellish the paper with pearlescent powdered pigments and glitter glue.

Create wings from artificial leaves accented with glitter. Attach to the center oval. Adhere the molded doll head with a strong adhesive. Beneath the doll head, adhere a button. To the bottom edge of frame, adhere a scalloped paper border, flower trim and self-adhesive pearls.

Faux Glass Tiles

The inspiration for these faux glass tiles came while I was on a trip to Buckhannon, West Virginia, a few summers ago. As I was watching some amazing glassblowing artisans at a glass factory, it came to me that I could re-create the look of handblown glass tiles using clear ultrathick embossing enamel and colored glass shards. The finished tiles came out even better than I imagined. Each is unique, as is all handblown glass, and can be used as wall art or decoration on box lids or attached to a bail as a beautiful charm for a necklace.

What You'll Need

Broken colored glass, patterned paper, clear ultrathick embossing enamel (UTEE), dimensional adhesive, two-part molding putty, gold-leafing pen, tweezers, scissors, melting pot

Tip

If you do not have colored broken glass pieces, color clear glass shards (found at most major craft stores) with alcohol inks. Be sure the alcohol inks are completely dry before using them with the melted ultrathick embossing enamel. Or go to a thrift store and purchase colored drinking glasses. They are inexpensive and easy to find.

1 Prepare the molding putty per step 1 of *Molded Embellishments*, page 73. Cut a 1½" (4cm) square from chipboard. Press the square into the putty to create a mold. Remove the chipboard.

2 Using tweezers, carefully place glass shards into the mold, making sure the prettiest side of the glass is facing down. Be very careful when handling the glass shards, as you do not want to cut yourself.

3 Heat the melting pot and clear ultrathick embossing enamel per the manufacturer's instructions. Once the UTEE is melted, carefully pour it over the glass pieces. Continue to pour the UTEE until the mold is filled. Set aside to let cool.

4 Once the enamel has cooled, remove the piece from the mold.

5 Apply dimensional adhesive to the back of the piece, then press the tile firmly onto patterned paper and let it all dry.

6 Once dry, use scissors to trim the excess paper from around the tile. Outline the edges of the tile with a gold-leafing pen.

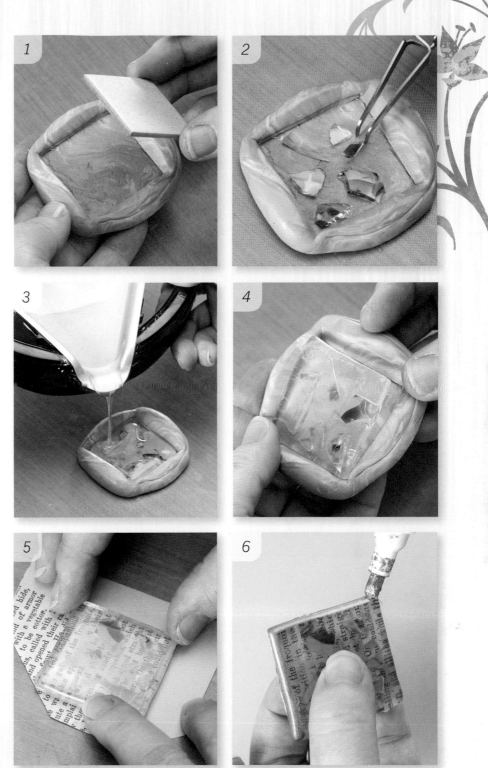

To finish this project, make a total of nine tiles. Use a palette knife to spread modeling paste over a 8" × 8" (20cm × 20cm) canvas. Gently press a rubber stamp into the paste (and clean your stamp as soon as you are done!). When the paste has dried, tint it with stains. Adhere a piece of lace vertically on the canvas. Cut a piece of cardboard to 5½" × 5½" (14cm × 14cm). Cover it with patterned paper and crackle paint. Adhere tiles to the cardboard piece with strong liquid adhesive, and use the same glue to adhere the cardboard to the canvas. After all of the pieces are set, add any embellishments you wish, such as a floral spray and ribbon.

Clay Flowers

The glass bowls I saw in Venice inspired this clay flower embellishment. The glass pieces there were simply stunning. I loved how the outer edges of some of the bowls showed beautiful movement, so I decided to duplicate that look with polymer clay. Once the clay was painted with Mica Gloss Metallic Effects Ink, it began to look like that Venetian glass. This flower made in a smaller size can be used as a charm to accent a necklace, a bracelet or even a ring. The technique remains the same, yet the possibilities for this flower are endless.

What You'll Need

Polymer clay (any color), circle templates in three sizes, metallic effects ink in five colors, hot glue sticks, hot glue gun, paintbrush, texture mat, pasta machine or brayer, oven

1 Roll the polymer clay to the desired thickness and cut three circles: small, medium and large. I used lids and bottoms of bottles of crafting supplies for my circle templates. Note that the clay color does not matter because you'll be painting it. From the flattened clay, cut out a square similar in size to the largest circle. Next roll a small ball of clay for the flower center.

2 Gently press each clay piece onto the texture mat. Carefully remove the clay from the texture mat.

3 Shape the edges of the circles by bending and pinching them, then bake the shapes according to the manufacturer's instructions.

4 Once baked and cooled, use a paintbrush to paint each circle with metallic effects ink and let dry. Then paint the back of each circle the same color and let dry.

5 Using a paintbrush, randomly apply a light metallic effects ink onto each of the three circles; let dry. Paint dark ink on the edges of each of the three circles; let dry. Apply metallic effects ink to the clay square and to the clay ball. Let dry. (I used green paint for the base, pearl for the highlight, brown for the dark, copper for the square and gold for the ball.)

6 Use a hot glue gun or strong liquid adhesive to adhere the circles on top of each other, starting with the largest circle first. Once the circles are attached, apply adhesive to the back of the clay ball and attach it to the center of the top clay circle. Let dry.

7 Adhere the flower to the center of the clay square.

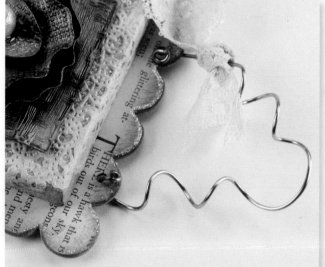

To finish this project, adhere patterned paper to the chipboard scalloped square with matte medium. Cut around the scallops with a craft knife to trim the paper. Rub the edges with sandpaper.

Apply ink over the edges of a chipboard square. Highlight the scallops with glitter glue. Use a heavy-duty punch to punch holes in the two upper corners of the scalloped square and one in the bottom center.

Coil the wire around a large paintbrush handle. Thread the ends of the wire through the top two holes and twist the wire ends to secure. Cut a strip of lace and tie it into a bow on the hanger. Attach a jump ring to a chandelier bead and attach the jump ring to the bottom hole.

Paint the mini canvas a color similar to the ink color used on the scalloped square and adhere a doily. Highlight the doily holes with glitter glue. Adhere the clay flower to the mini canvas using strong liquid adhesive.

Clay Embellishments

Vintage carnival and goofus glass were the inspirations behind these embellishments. Mom and I love almost every kind of vintage glass, but neither of us is fond of goofus glass—Mom *really* doesn't like it. She had a goofus glass vase in the late 1960s, and she actually peeled off all the red and gold paint. So when I painted the rose-embossed heart red and gold, I instantly thought of Mom. The other hearts look more like carnival glass because I used many colors of Mica Gloss Ink on them. Once the clear embossing powder is applied, the hearts really resemble vintage glass embellishments.

What You'll Need

Polymer clay, metallic effects ink in two colors, embossing ink, clear embossing powder, heart paper punch, paintbrush, texture mat, pasta machine or brayer, heat tool, oven

1 Roll the clay thin enough to slide into a punch. Punch out the heart.

2 Place the punched heart onto a texture mat and press gently. Carefully remove the heart from the mat.

3 Bake the clay according to the manufacturer's instructions. Once cooled, use a paintbrush to apply metallic effects ink to the roses; apply the second ink color randomly to the background. Let dry.

4 Apply embossing ink to the front of the heart.

5 Generously apply clear embossing powder to the ink.

6 Tap off the excess powder. Using a heat tool, heat the embossing powder until it melts. While the melted powder is still hot, sprinkle additional clear embossing powder onto the heart and heat again until melted.

To finish this project, create two full hearts and one partial heart. To create the word strip, roll out the clay onto a nonstick craft sheet. Using rubber stamps, stamp each letter into the clay. Use a craft knife to carefully trim around the word, and bake it according to the manufacturer's instructions. Once cool, use a paintbrush and metallic effects ink to paint each letter; paint the background, and let dry. Follow steps 4–6 to apply embossing powder to the word strip.

Ink the larger canvas. While wet, sprinkle embossing powder onto the canvas, and heat to melt it. Punch a scallop border from metal foil tape and adhere it to the canvas corners. (Remove excess metal foil tape from inside the punch after each use.) Paint the smaller canvas, and while the paint is still wet, use a stylus to incise marks. Accent these marks with a gel pen. Adhere the small canvas to the larger canvas using strong liquid adhesive. Adhere the hearts, then adhere the word strip to a heart.

Faux Enamel

I believe this is one of my favorite techniques. It's simple to do, and the results are stunning. The secret to achieving the faux enameled patina is to use several different colors of embossing powder. Multiple earth tones help create a perfectly aged look. This charm looks as though it fell from a necklace years ago and has been newly discovered.

What You'll Need

Metal spoon (flattened, with handle removed), embossing powders in four colors, microbeads in three colors, enameling resin, heat-resistant nonstick craft sheet, nonstick craft sheet, melting pot, drill

1 Drill a small hole into the top of the spoon. Place the spoon onto a heat-resistant nonstick craft sheet. Place the melting pot on a craft sheet, and place the heat-resistant nonstick craft sheet into the melting pot. Set to medium heat, place the lid on the pot and let the spoon absorb the heat.

2 Once the spoon is hot, sprinkle embossing powders onto the spoon and let them melt. I used green, dark gold, copper and light gold.

3 Squeeze enameling resin from the bottle onto the spoon. Let the resin melt. Continue to add resin until the entire front of the spoon is covered.

4 Sprinkle the microbeads into the melted resin. If you wish to accent your spoon with other items, such as beads, buttons, or rhinestones, add them at this time while the resin is hot. Add more resin on top of the items and let it melt.

5 Carefully remove the craft sheet from the melting pot, place it onto a nonstick craft sheet and allow the spoon to cool.

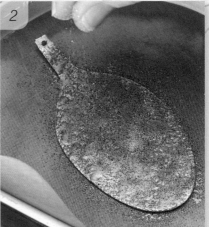

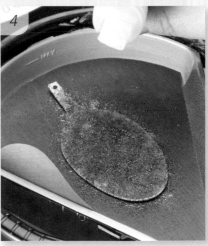

Tip

Some colored embossing powders have a white base; if they are heated too long, the color will melt off and the embossing powder will go back to the original white. To prevent this, either use embossing powders that have a clear base, or work quickly when applying embossing powders to your metal item.

To finish this project, repeat the process of faux enameling with a leaf charm. Insert one jump ring through the hole in the spoon and one through the hole in the leaf. To the spoon's jump ring, attach the leaf charm, a bead dangle and two additional beads. Use the technique featured in *Stamped Metal*, pages 56–59, to create the metal stamped word strips from copper sheeting. Attach the metal strips to the spoon with strong liquid adhesive.

Resin Charm

Charm bracelets are one of my favorite accessories. I wanted this bracelet to have an eclectic feel, so I pulled out all shapes and sizes of vintage buttons and cuff links, copper and silver charms and this silver shield pendant. Again, I never worry about mixing silver, copper and gold—I like the look! Since a bracelet is not complete for me unless it has a little sparkle, I added the small strip of rhinestone trim inside the shield. With a resin project like this, I wait 48 hours after the hard cure stage before I wear it.

What You'll Need

Pendant with raised sides, rhinestone trim, beads, two-part liquid resin, disposable mixing cup, craft stick, disposable gloves, tweezers, plastic straw or heat tool (optional)

Tip

If you have resin left over after this project, make resin paper by following the technique described in *Resin Paper*, pages 110–111.

1 While wearing disposable gloves, place equal parts of resin and hardener into a mixing cup.

2 Stir the parts using a craft stick for 2 minutes; be sure to time how long you stir, as it's key to the resin curing properly. Set the resin aside to allow the bubbles to rise and pop.

3 While the resin is degassing, place the rhinestone trim and beads into the pendant.

4 If any bubbles remain in the resin, blow over them through a straw or carefully give them a few blasts from a heat tool. Scoop resin onto the craft stick and let it fall freely into the pendant. Continue to add resin until the pendant is filled.

Place the pendant on a flat surface in a dust-free area or cover the pendant with a cup. Allow the charm to cure for at least 12 hours before moving it. After 12 hours, the resin will be at a soft cure; it will be at a hard cure in 24 hours.

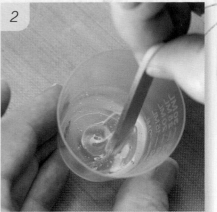

Tip

If you are new to measuring resin, use one cup to measure the resin and another to measure the hardener. Then pour the hardener in with the resin and mix as instructed by the manufacturer.

To create a decal transfer, punch out an image from a sheet of transfer decals. Place the decal into a bowl of room-temperature water and let it soak for 1 minute. Remove and blot the decal with a paper towel, then slide the decal image onto your charm. Using a paper towel, blot any additional water off the decal while pressing lightly to remove any air bubbles. Using a paintbrush, apply a thin layer of sealant over the dried image. Let dry. You can leave the charm as is or apply a layer of dimensional adhesive or resin.

To finish this project, use jump rings to attach as many and whatever type of beads, charms and embellishments you desire to a purchased chain. Use the technique featured in *Stamped Metal*, pages 56–59, to stamp words into any of the metal charms. I added fifty buttons, beads, dangles and charms.

Faux Porcelain Flowers

Every flower I picked as a child and handed to my mom and grandmothers is the inspiration behind this piece. In my eyes, a blooming morning glory and blooming weed were equally beautiful. Seeing the flowers I picked displayed prominently on the kitchen table in a juice glass or small vase was so exciting to me. Something about a small bouquet of flowers handpicked by a child melts my heart.

What You'll Need

Clear ultrathick embossing enamel (UTEE), paper flowers and leaves, nonstick craft sheet, melting pot

1 Place your melting pot on a nonstick craft sheet and turn the thermostat to the UTEE setting. Pour clear UTEE into the melting pot and replace the lid to allow the UTEE to melt completely. Carefully place your paper flower into the melted UTEE and turn it to completely coat the flower.

2 Remove the flower from the pot and let the excess drip away. While the UTEE is dripping from the flower, gently rotate the flower until it is cool enough to place onto your nonstick craft sheet without making a puddle.

3 Repeat with the other paper flowers and leaves.

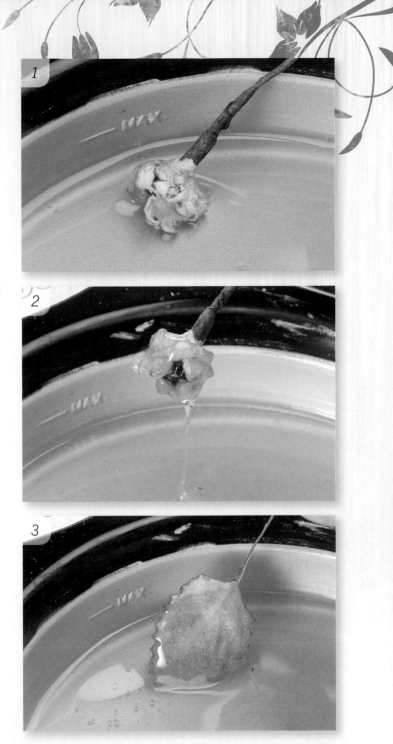

To finish this project, coat four flowers, four roses and three leaves with UTEE. Wrap a wooden spool with patterned paper. Adhere a doily to the bottom of the spool. Stamp a metal charm (see *Stamped Metal*, pages 56–59) and attach a jump ring to it. Stamp a strip of muslin with rubber stamps and black ink. Tie the muslin around the spool and add the stamped metal charm as you tie the final knot. Insert the flowers into the hole in the spool and secure with glue, if necessary.

Trim around the words of a sentiment printed on paper and ink the edges. Insert the paper into the memo clip and tie a piece of embroidery floss around the clip. Insert into the hole in the spool.

Jewelry Clay Butterfly

When creating, I have a tendency to leave my baubles out in between projects. They remain on my worktable, close by, and I add them to projects as I create. I figure, "Why put them away when I'm just going to pull them back out again?" This collage piece was inspired when several vintage buttons, beads, cuff links and rhinestones came together in a grouping that resembled a butterfly. The way I see it, fate was stepping in here, and I had to go with the inspiration.

What You'll Need

Chipboard shape, two-part jewelry clay, pearlescent powdered pigments, dry brush, long resin or jewelry piece, assorted buttons and beads, microbeads, disposable gloves

1 Wearing disposable gloves, form equal-sized balls of jewelry clay, one ball from each container. Mix the two balls together for 2 minutes.

2 Completely cover the front of the chipboard butterfly with the jewelry clay.

3 With a dry brush, apply pearlescent pigment powder to the clay shape.

4 Press a long resin piece onto the center of the butterfly to resemble its body. Then add buttons and beads until the entire front has been covered.

5 To fill in the spaces between the beads and buttons, pour microbeads into a shallow bowl and press the butterfly into the microbeads.

Turn the butterfly over and shake gently to remove any excess beads. Set aside to cure for 24 to 48 hours.

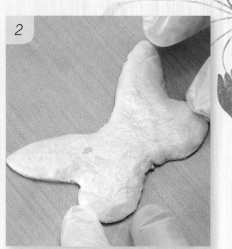

Tip

You can repeat these same steps on smaller chipboard shapes to create charms for necklaces, bracelet embellishments and rings.

To finish this project, paint a mini canvas. Cut a piece of patterned paper a bit smaller than the canvas. Ink the edges of the patterned paper and adhere it to the canvas, leaving a bit of the canvas showing around the edges. Paint crackle paint on the paper. Adhere the butterfly to the canvas with strong liquid adhesive.

Chapter Four

Paper

I have a true love for any and all kinds of vintage paper. And that's what this chapter is all about—creating with pages from old books and sheet music, ledger paper with beautiful handwritten notes, tattered wallpaper and, of course, current patterned papers in the vintage style I love so much. To me, there is nothing prettier than aged papers because they feature so many beautiful shades of creams and browns. So, no matter the condition of any papers you may stumble upon during your vintage shopping, grab them because you can use them in so many ways—and I am ready to show you a few! In this chapter, you will learn how to turn vintage images from old magazines into unique pieces of jewelry and how to turn sheet music into lovely leaves to accent a wildflower assemblage. You will also see how I used patterned paper for a modern take on a dream catcher that is perfect to hang in any little girl's room.

Paper Feather

Even though this canvas is filled with lots of different items, I wanted to keep the main focus on the feathers. So I used muted acrylic paint colors in cream and soft pink to cover the center of the canvas. Silver glass glitter on the top and bottom of the canvas helps accent the glitter on the feathers, bringing the focus back to where I want it to be.

What You'll Need

Thin patterned paper, feather template on page 118, seam binding, floral wire or 20-gauge wire, pencil, glitter glue, strong liquid adhesive, scissors, wire cutters

1 Using a pencil, trace the feather template onto paper. Cut out the feather. With wire cutters, cut a piece of floral wire to about 1" (3cm) longer than the paper feather.

2 Apply a very thin line of liquid adhesive along the center of the paper feather. Place the wire on top of the adhesive.

3 Turn the feather over and use your fingers to carefully pinch along both sides of the wire, allowing the paper to attach around the wire. If you like, you can wrap a strip of paper around the wire stem, as well.

4 With scissors, snip along both sides of the feather, cutting just to the wire.

5 Slightly bend some of the snipped paper to add texture to the feather. Apply glitter glue down the center of the feather and along the feather's edges. Let dry.

6 Tie a small piece of seam binding to the base of the feather.

To finish this project, create a second paper feather, and tie the two together with the seam binding. Cut paper to cover the top and sides of the canvas, and adhere with matte medium. Paint the paper with transparent layers of pink and cream paint. When dry, paint scallops at the top and bottom of the canvas. When dry, outline the scallops with charcoal pencil and smudge the line a bit with your finger. Brush crackle paint over the surface.

Apply modeling paste through the holes of a polka-dot stencil. Allow to dry. Highlight the dots with pink powdered pigment and glitter glue. Apply a thin line of liquid adhesive to the top and bottom edges of the canvas. Dip each glued edge in glass glitter. Accent with buttons and a stamped message, outlined with charcoal pencil if desired. Adhere feathers to the canvas with adhesive foam dots.

Accented Papers

When I make a three-dimensional collage like this one, I think of the piece as a creative puzzle. I find true joy in discovering items that fit perfectly in the spaces and layers on the canvas. Collages are fun because you can incorporate any type of embellishment—and I do use anything. Vintage shell and metal buttons are great to fill in space and add texture. Rhinestone trim and vintage pearls add color and sparkle. So when you go to a flea market, take a peek inside all the little bags and boxes to find a wide array of items that are perfect to use in your three-dimensional collages.

What You'll Need

1½" × 1½" (4cm × 4cm) chipboard square, patterned paper, rhinestone trim, acrylic stamp, ink, glitter glue, glue stick, strong liquid adhesive, scissors

1 Apply glue stick adhesive to your chipboard square. Place the patterned paper on top and press down to secure the paper in place. Trim the paper around the chipboard with scissors or a craft knife and mat.

2 Ink a stamp with archival ink and stamp the image onto the paper.

3 Embellish the square with rhinestone trim, adhering it with strong liquid adhesive.

4 Accent the stamped image using glitter glue. Let dry.

Tip

Use the blank margins from old books to write or stamp onto. Vintage books have beautifully aged pages, which means perfectly aged tones, too. When I have margin scraps left over from projects, I toss them into a box next to my worktable for future use. You can do the same thing on the edges of sheet music, too.

To finish this project, cover the scalloped-edge chipboard background with patterned paper, and trim the paper from around the scallops. Paint the paper with crackle paint. Ink the edges of the scallops to distress them. Accent the edges of the scallops with gold paint.

Attach metal edging to the bottom edge of a 5" × 7" (13cm × 18cm) canvas. Cover the canvas with patterned paper; distress with ink, then outline the edges with paint or ink. Cut a piece of burlap slightly smaller than the canvas and glue it to the top. Adhere this piece to the scalloped piece with adhesive foam dots.

Create several more chipboard embellishments as described above. Arrange them and add embellishments, including buttons with knotted embroidery floss, game pieces, keys and flowers, as desired.

Photo Silhouette

I've always had a love for silhouettes, whether they picture chubby-faced babies, men, women or ornate scenes. You can find pretty framed silhouette art in antique stores—usually at a pretty price. So I decided to create my own silhouette art using family photos. If it's not convenient for you to scan and print your own photos to use as templates, you can find lots of vintage photos at flea markets, thrift shops and antique stores. You can cut the image out of the photo and use it as a template, or you can flip the image over for a silhouette in a beautifully aged cream color.

What You'll Need

Image of person or people, cardstock, pencil, scissors, craft knife, cutting mat

1 Print a family photo to the size needed for your canvas. Do not worry about the quality of the image; all you need is the outline of the people or person to make the silhouette. Using scissors, cut around the image of the people as closely as possible. Place the image onto a cutting mat and use a craft knife to cut the areas in between the people's arms and legs or between groups.

2 Place the silhouette onto black cardstock and use a pencil to lightly trace the silhouette.

3 Using scissors, cut around the traced image. Again, use the craft knife to cut any small areas.

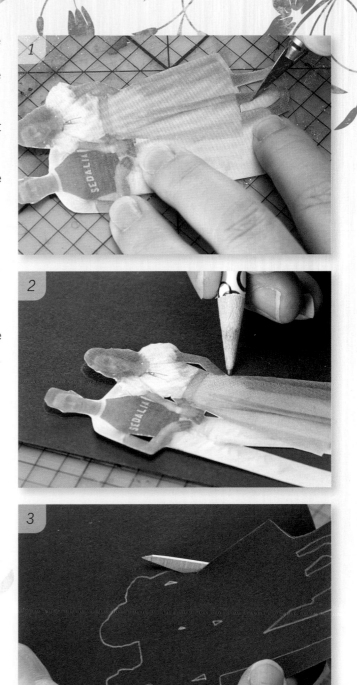

To finish this project, follow the instructions on pages 100–103 to create a *Canvas Paper Transfer*. Cover the sides of the 4" × 4" (10cm × 10cm) canvas with paper. Adhere the canvas transfer to the top. Glue stamped words of your choice to the canvas. Adhere the silhouette to the canvas with adhesive foam dots for height and dimension.

Cut four pieces of aluminum metal foil tape to the length needed to cover each of the top edges of the canvas. Using scallop scissors, trim the foil tape along one long edge. Attach the foil tape to the canvas so the straight edge of the tape folds over the canvas edge just slightly. Once all four edges of the canvas are covered with the scalloped foil tape, add detailing to the tape with a stylus.

Charms From Vintage Papers

Looking through some magazines from the early 1920s, I was taken with the beauty of all the ladies and their gorgeous hats and stylish shoes. I thought it would be wonderful to preserve some of these images in simple charms. Scanning and printing the images using a laser printer allows you to preserve the magazine and still create items using its artwork and wording. Aluminum metal foil tape provides a simple way to create a faux-soldered look for your piece, too. Metal foil tape also comes in brass and copper finishes.

What You'll Need

1" (3cm) wooden square, metal jewelry bail, image, computer paper, ink, gold-leafing pen, two-part resin, disposable cups, craft stick, aluminum metal foil tape, glue stick, clear-drying glue, E6000, paintbrush, pinking shears, scissors, laser printer

1 Scan a vintage, copyright-free illustration from a magazine, and print it onto computer paper using a laser printer. Using a glue stick, apply glue to the wooden square and place it on the back of the printed illustration. Press firmly to adhere.

2 Trim around the square with scissors. Ink the edges of the square for a distressed look. Ink the entire image lightly, if desired.

3 Apply clear-drying glue to the top of the paper image with a brush and let dry. Repeat this step three times. The glue seals the image and protects it from the resin you'll add later.

4 Accent the edges of the square with a gold-leafing pen.

5 Mix the jewelry resin according to the manufacturer's instructions. Carefully pour the resin onto the paper image, making sure the resin covers the image. Use a craft stick to spread the resin as needed. Place your charm on a level surface in a dust-free area. Let the charm sit for 24 hours to cure. (See *Resin Charm*, pages 84–85 for more on using resin.)
　Cut four pieces of aluminum metal foil tape slightly longer than the sides of wooden square. Using pinking shears, cut one straight edge of the foil tape. Peel the paper backing off the tape and attach the tape to one side of the charm. Continue this step until all four sides are covered with the foil tape.

6 Using E6000, attach a bail to the back of the wooden square to create a charm.

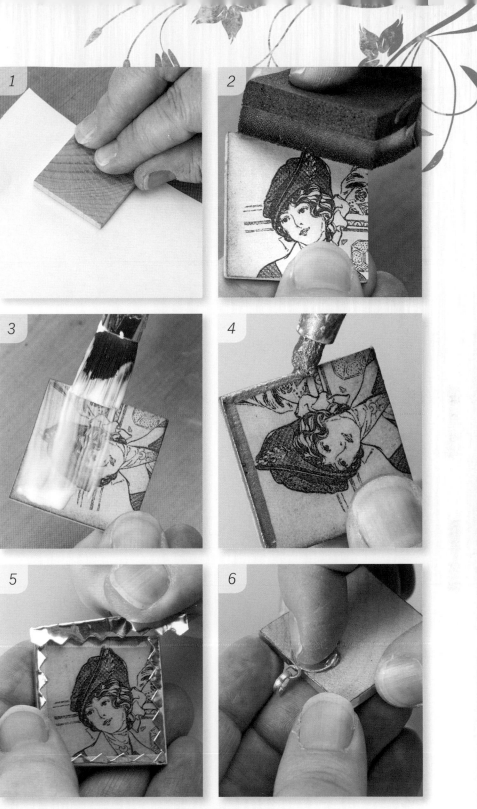

To finish this project, attach a rhinestone button and pearl bead chain to the bail with jump rings.

Canvas Paper Transfer

Vintage wallpaper is something I really love. I find the textures, designs and colors so inspiring and perfect to use in collages. If you find a patterned paper that reminds you of vintage wallpaper, you can easily add texture to the paper—as well as a distressed feel—by transferring it to adhesive canvas. Once you complete the transfer, you end up with a canvas-textured image that is ready to use in any project. This type of image transfer is perfect to sew onto fabric totes and other fabric items as well. You can even use metal dies to cut the canvas into shapes.

What You'll Need

Bird and wing die or stencil, adhesive canvas, patterned paper, glitter glue, ink, matte medium, blending tool (optional), mist bottle filled with water, brayer, scissors, die cut machine

1 Using a template and scissors or a die cut machine, cut out a bird and a wing from the adhesive canvas. You will use the sticky side of the canvas for the front of your bird, so make sure to cut the bird facing in the desired direction. Peel the backing off of the adhesive canvas.

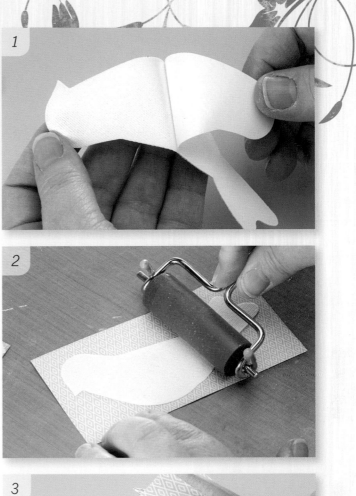

2 Attach each adhesive canvas piece to the front of a piece of patterned paper, pressing the paper down firmly. You may want to use a brayer to ensure the paper is secure.

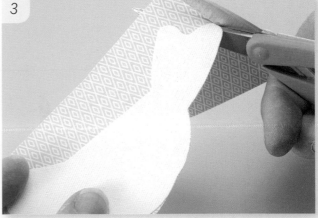

3 Using scissors, trim the shapes from the patterned paper.

4 Mist water over the back of the shapes. You want to completely wet the back of the patterned paper.

5 Use your finger to gently rub off the back of the paper until you see the patterned paper underneath. Continue to add water while rubbing off the paper if needed.

6 Once all the paper backing is removed, apply a small amount of matte medium to the shape with your finger to get rid of any small remaining pieces of paper.

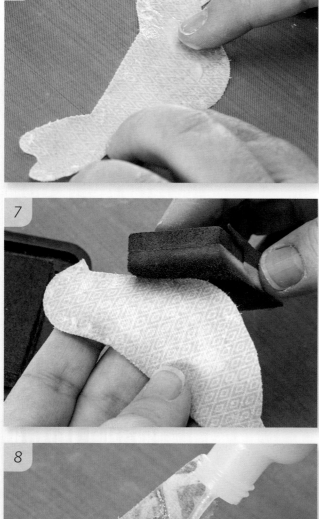

7 Apply ink to the edges of the bird's body and wing using a blending tool, if desired.

8 Outline the bird with glitter glue, then use the glitter glue to outline the wing and accent it further, as desired.

Tips

Mitering paper pieces is something I like to do to give my projects a more polished feel. I cut all the pieces to the size needed and place them on top of the canvas where I will attach them permanently once all the edges are cut.

Work from left to right and begin with the left vertical paper piece and top horizontal paper piece. Align the papers so their ends match up correctly, forming an upside down **L**.

With scissors, begin cutting from the inside corner of the **L**, and cut a straight line to the outer point (or the outer corner of the **L**).

Move on to the next corner, matching up the ends of the top horizontal paper piece with the right vertical paper, and cut as before. Repeat these steps until all of the corners have been cut. Glue the pieces into place.

When using larger pieces of paper, use a repositionable adhesive to keep the pieces in place while you cut. Once all the edges have been cut, use an adhesive eraser to remove the unwanted adhesive.

To finish this piece, follow steps 2–6 to transfer patterned paper to a piece of 5" × 5" (13cm × 13cm) adhesive canvas.

Adhere patterned paper to a chipboard frame. Using a floral stamp, stamp the paper with embossing ink, sprinkle with embossing powder and heat to melt. Apply paint over the embossed frame and use a paper towel to lightly remove paint from the embossed areas. Glue the canvas square inside the frame.

Using a ruler stamp and black archival ink, stamp the scalloped chipboard border. Sprinkle the inked area with clear powder and heat to emboss it. Apply paint over the embossed border and use a damp paper towel to lightly remove the paint from the embossed area. Adhere the border to the frame.

Apply embossing ink to the chipboard letters. Sprinkle on gold embossing powder and just barely heat it, so the powder retains some of its texture.

Paint the chipboard flower with different colors of crackle paint; when dry, embellish with glitter glue. Adhere the flower and the letters to the canvas. Adhere the wing to the bird. Place the bird on the canvas with adhesive foam dots.

Faux Resin Leaves

I love the sight of wildflowers along the roadside during a Texas spring. Seeing little pops of color sway as cars pass by brightens my day. When I decided to reproduce this memory into a canvas collage, I knew I wanted to use vintage papers because the aged cream tones would highlight the pops of color on the flowers. But I wanted the background to be dimensional and interesting, too. Finally it hit me: Rolled pieces of book pages would do the trick. I am thrilled with the outcome, as the book pages create a dimensional, yet subtle background, perfect to show off my wildflower art piece.

What You'll Need

Patterned paper, 16-gauge wire, clear-drying liquid adhesive, dimensional adhesive, hot glue sticks and hot glue gun or E6000, straight pin, craft knife, cutting mat, wire cutters

1 Using wire cutters, cut a piece of 16-gauge silver wire to about 5" (13cm) long. Bend each end of the wire toward the center of the wire.

2 Continue bending the wire ends until they touch the center of the wire and form two loops.

3 Apply clear-drying glue to the back of the looped wire.

4 Attach the wire to the front of a piece of patterned paper.

Tip

You can use wallpaper, sheet music or any kind of patterned paper that can be rolled to create this background.

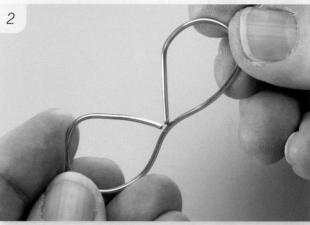

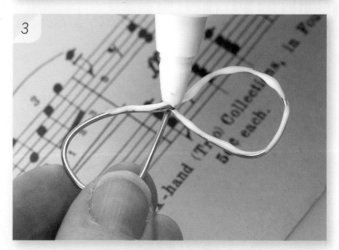

5 Once the adhesive is dry, cover the paper and fill in the loops with dimensional adhesive. Keep a straight pin handy to pop any bubbles that might form. Set the leaves aside to dry.

6 Place the paper on a cutting mat and use a craft knife to cut the excess paper from around the wire leaves. You can cut with scissors, if you prefer, but you can get closer to the wire with a craft knife.

Using wire cutters, cut a piece of 16-gauge wire to the length you want your flower stem. Using E6000 or hot glue, attach the leaves to the stem of your flower. Once the leaves are securely attached to the stem, bend the leaves a bit to give dimension to your finished piece.

To finish this piece, create seven leaf sets and cut the flower stems to various lengths.

Paint the top and sides of the 4" × 12" (10cm × 30cm) canvas. Randomly stamp the canvas with a text stamp.

Tear a book page or patterned paper in half horizontally and place it on your work surface with a corner at the top center and bottom center, like a diamond. Starting at the bottom, roll the paper to form a tube shape.

Attach the tube to the canvas with hot glue, making sure the seam side is down. Repeat these steps until the entire front of the canvas is covered with rolled paper. Lightly apply white gesso over the rolled paper with a paintbrush.

Randomly apply matte medium to the rolled paper and sprinkle coarse glitter on top. Tap off the excess glitter and let dry.

Using a handheld punch, punch seven flowers from an aluminum can (see *Soda Can Flowers*, pages 50–53). Paint the flowers and then distress them a bit with steel wool. Using hot glue, add buttons with knotted embroidery floss to the centers of the flowers. Adhere one flower to each wire stem with hot glue. When the glue is dry, arrange the flowers on top of the rolled paper. Once you like your arrangement, carefully adhere the stems to the paper using strong liquid adhesive.

Patchwork Background

I love old hand-stitched quilts, and my family is fortunate to have several created by my Grandmother Childers and great-great-aunts Minnie and Mandy Childers. It amazes me how each precise stitch was placed on the beautiful fabric pieces that were either store-bought or cut from feed sacks. Grungepaper, a thick cardstock, allows you to create embossed images that make a perfect faux-quilted background. This type of background is easy to ink, paint, highlight and distress.

What You'll Need

Grungepaper, acrylic paint, pearlescent pigment powders in three colors, computer paper, paintbrush, sandpaper, thread, tape runner, embossing machine, embossing dies, paper trimmer, scissors, sewing machine

1 Using a paper trimmer, cut the Grungepaper into four 2" (5cm) squares. With an embossing machine, emboss two of the squares with each of two dies (I used polka dots and flowers).

Paint the four embossed squares with acrylic paint, and let dry. Sand the embossed areas of each square to add highlights.

2 Wet a paintbrush with water and accent the embossed areas with pearlescent powdered pigments. Let dry.

3 Cut the embossed squares into four 1" (3cm) squares.

Cut a piece of computer paper to 3½" (9cm) square. Using a tape runner, apply adhesive to the back of each embossed square, and attach to the 3½" (9cm) square. The paper will be smaller than the patchwork.

With a sewing machine and cream thread, sew a zigzag stitch in between each of the horizontal rows, then stitch between all the vertical rows. Sew a straight stitch around the outer edge of the square.

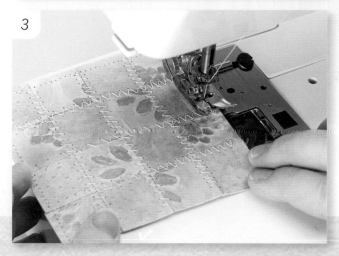

4 Distress the edges with a paper distresser or by running the blade of your scissors along the edge.

To finish this project, paint the top and sides of a 4" × 4" (10cm × 10cm) gallery-wrapped canvas. Adhere the patchwork square to the canvas using strong liquid adhesive.

Punch butterfly shapes from patterned paper and ink the edges. Stack the butterflies and stitch through the center of the body, leaving a tail of threads. Fold the layers of wings and adhere the bottom butterfly to the patchwork background.

Use metal stamp letters to hammer a word onto a piece of Grungepaper. Highlight the text and draw a border using a gold permanent marker. Cut out the text and adhere it to your patchwork background.

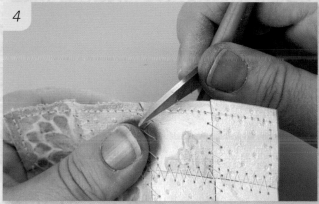

Resin Paper

This canvas came together in bits and pieces. I knew I wanted to use butterflies punched from resin paper, but I really had no idea where to go from there. I looked at quotes online for inspiration, and once I found this quote by Ida Rentoul Outhwaite, inspiration hit. Before I knew it, I was painting, punching, stitching and glittering, and I ended up with this sweet canvas. Creating really is a journey, so don't fight it—just keep adding the items you love and enjoy the process.

What You'll Need

Two-part resin, patterned paper, self-adhesive pearls, disposable gloves, disposable mixing cup, craft stick, disposable paintbrush, plastic wrap, paper punch

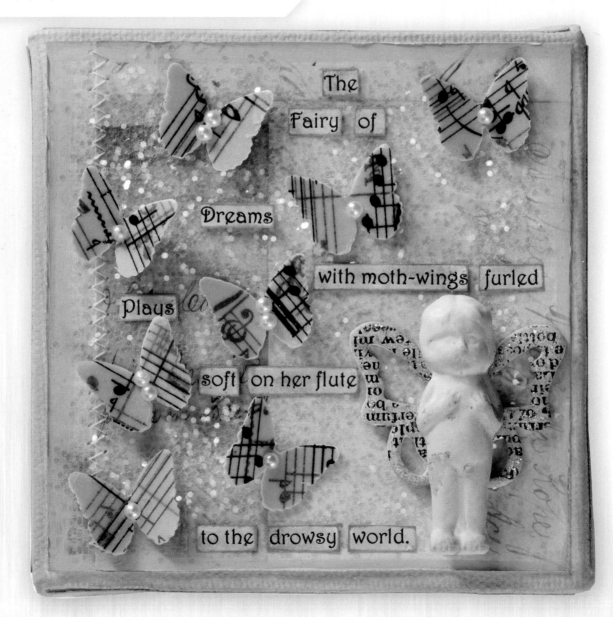

1 Wearing disposable gloves, mix the resin according to the manufacturer's instructions. Note: It is very important that your resin cures in a room not lower than 70° F (21° C). If the temperature is too cold, the resin will not cure properly.

Place a piece of plastic wrap onto your work surface and set a piece of patterned paper on it.

Using a disposable paint-brush, apply the resin to the top of the paper. Once the paper is covered, turn it over and apply resin to the back.

2 Allow the resin to cure for 24 hours. Once it has cured, punch the butterfly shapes for your project using a butterfly punch.

3 Accent the punched butter-flies with self-adhesive pearls.

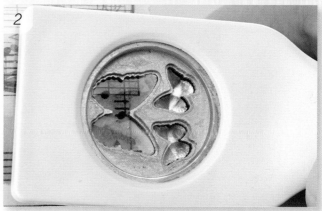

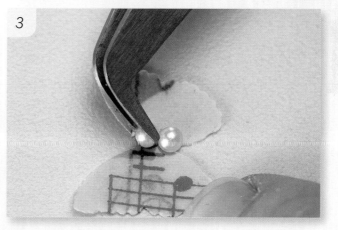

Tip

Whenever I have leftover resin, no matter how little, I create resin paper to use in future projects. This way I have a little stash of resin paper at the ready, and I don't have to wait the 24-hour curing time to complete a project.

To finish this project, make a total of eight resin butterflies and add pearls to each.

Paint the top and sides of the mini canvas. When dry, adhere patterned paper to the sides and distress with more paint.

Create a collage of paper for the top of the canvas, stitching some papers together and distressing with paint. Adhere the collage to the top of the canvas. Spread matte medium over the canvas and sprinkle with coarse crystal glitter. Let dry.

Adhere the resin paper butterflies with strong liquid adhesive. Paint the chipboard butterfly, and when dry, use black archival ink and a text stamp to stamp the butterfly. Apply glitter.

Adhere the butterfly to the canvas, and glue a molded doll on top of the butterfly with strong liquid adhesive (see *Molded Embellishments*, pages 72–73 for instructions on making the molded doll). Cut out the words of your sentiment, ink their edges and adhere them to the canvas.

Decoupage Papier-Mâché

The papier-mâché bird on this canvas is actually half of a decorative box. When I found the package of three bird boxes, I saw six birds that I could alter in all kinds of different ways. I decided to decoupage, paint and stamp this one, but I have ideas to cover the others with fabric, mists, modeling paste and glitter. Just because an item is meant for one thing doesn't mean that's how you have to use it. Keep this in mind when you peruse the clearance aisles, as most items can be used as a base for an altered project.

What You'll Need

Papier-mâché shape, sewing pattern tissue, acrylic paint in two colors, ink, glitter glue, matte medium, unmounted acrylic stamp, charcoal pencil, paintbrushes

1 Using a paintbrush, apply matte medium to the top of the papier-mâché bird. Place sewing pattern tissue on top of the wet medium. Brush over the tissue with more matte medium to secure it in place. Repeat these steps until you achieve the coverage you like.

2 Tuck the excess tissue inside the back of the bird.

3 Apply a thin coat of paint to the bird, and let dry.

4 Accent the wing, tail, belly and top of the bird's head with gold metallic acrylic paint, and let dry.

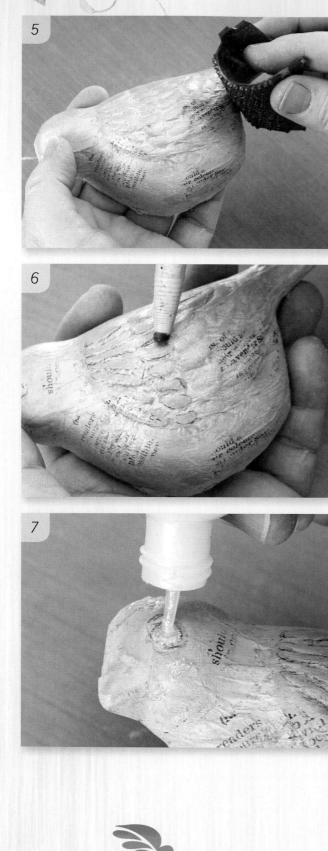

5 Ink an unmounted acrylic stamp and stamp randomly over the bird. The unmounted stamp allows you to stamp the curved areas of the bird and looks more random.

6 Define the bird's wing and tail feathers, eye and beak using a charcoal pencil.

7 Apply glitter glue to your finger and rub it onto the bird's head and belly. Apply some to the eye directly from the bottle. Let dry.

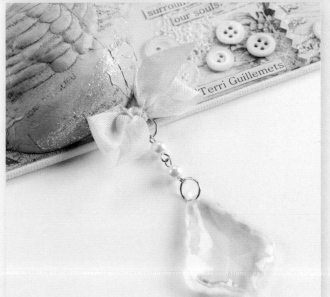

To finish this project, create a collage with patterned papers, a paper doily, buttons, a key and glitter glue. Adhere the collage to a 5" × 7" (13cm × 18cm) canvas.

Create a banner by cutting triangles from Grungepaper or chipboard. Emboss the shapes with polka dots, distress them with ink and accent the dots with glitter glue. Use metal stamps to stamp the letters into the Grungepaper. Cut out each letter and distress them. Adhere one letter to each pendant with strong liquid adhesive. Thread baker's twine through the holes in the banner and adhere the twine to the canvas.

Attach a large jump ring to each end of a pearl bead chain. From one jump ring, attach a chandelier bead. Tie a seam binding bow to the other jump ring and glue the seam binding to the canvas with fabric adhesive. Adhere the bird to the canvas. Cut around the words of your sentiment. Ink the paper to distress it and then glue it to the canvas.

Spool Tassel

This mini wall hanging is my personal take on a dream catcher. This dream catcher was created to catch all of the dreams and wishes of the owner. To me, little girls and butterflies just seem to go together, so that is what I decided to use as the base for this piece. Of course you can use any shape for your background. This dream catcher would not be complete without a pretty, flowy tassle made of ribbons and repeating the butterfly theme.

What You'll Need

Wooden spool, patterned paper, seam binding in three colors, screw eye, pearl bead chain, acrylic paint, 20-gauge wire, paintbrush, hot glue sticks, hot glue gun, strong liquid adhesive, scissors, wire cutters

1 Paint a wooden spool with acrylic paint; let dry. Cut a piece of patterned paper to wrap around the spool and attach with adhesive.

2 Using scissors, cut two 6" (15cm) pieces of seam binding in each of three different colors, for a total of six pieces.

Cut a piece of 20-gauge wire to 4"(10cm) in length with wire cutters. Hold all six pieces of seam binding at one end and wrap the wire around the end of the seam binding.

3 Apply a small amount of hot glue to the inside bottom of the wooden spool. Insert the wrapped seam binding, making sure the wrapped wire does not show.

4 Apply a small amount of hot glue to the inside top of the wooden spool, and insert a screw eye.

5 Attach a small pearl bead chain to the screw eye.

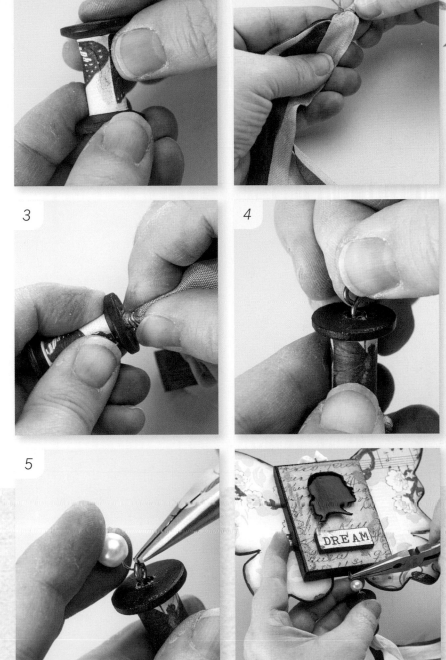

To finish this project, adhere patterned paper to a butterfly chipboard shape. Sand and ink the edges of the paper, accent with glitter glue and paint the edges of the chipboard with paint.

Paint the mini canvas on the top and sides. Screw in two screw eyes, one at the top center of the canvas, the other at the bottom center.

Adhere paper to the top of the canvas, then apply crackle paint and let dry. Randomly apply modeling paste to the paper. Once dry, wet a paintbrush with water and apply pigment powder to the embossed area.

Paint the chipboard silhouette with black acrylic paint. When dry, apply embossing ink and sprinkle on clear embossing powder. Melt the embossing powder with a heat tool. Adhere the shape to the center of the canvas with an adhesive foam dot.

Paint the edges of a chipboard scrap, and adhere a stamped or printed word when dry. Glue the chipboard word to the canvas. Adhere the canvas to the butterfly shape. Tie seam binding through the top screw eye for hanging. Attach the spool to the bottom screw eye with a loop from the pearl bead chain.

Patterns

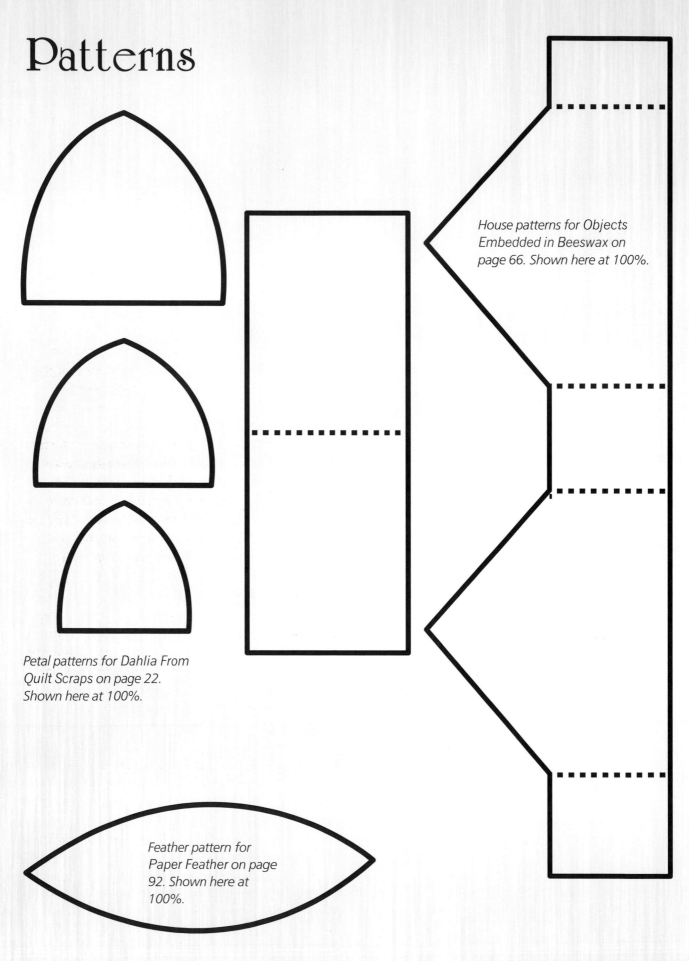

House patterns for Objects Embedded in Beeswax on page 66. Shown here at 100%.

Petal patterns for Dahlia From Quilt Scraps on page 22. Shown here at 100%.

Feather pattern for Paper Feather on page 92. Shown here at 100%.

Complete Project Materials Lists

If you'd like to make the projects as I have, below you'll find the complete materials lists for each project in this book. Note that many of the items I use in my art are found at flea markets and antique shops, so you may need to substitute your own amazing finds.

Chapter One

Bird's Nest

7" × 9" (18cm × 23cm) canvas; ladle; patterned paper; chenille fabric; crochet trim, daisy trim, brown velvet trim (Maya Road); yarn; embroidery floss; beads; shell buttons; fabric leaf (Laura's Vintage Garden); earring; seam binding; beads; chandelier beads (Maya Road); Dresden trim (Collage Stuff); memo pin (Advantus); Scrabble game pieces; ink (Vintage Photo Distress Ink by Ranger); hot glue sticks; hot glue gun; sewing needle; paper trimmer; scissors

Felted Heart

5" × 5" (13cm × 13cm) canvas; zipper trim (Maya Road); wool felt; wool roving in two colors; embroidery floss; beads; doilies and lace (Laura's Vintage Garden); shell buttons; muslin; fabric adhesive; pencil; scissors; embroidery needle; needle-felting pen; brush needle-felting pad

Textile Cuff

Quilt pieces; lace trims, textile flower, pearl bead chain, rhinestone trim (Maya Road); doilies, satin button (Laura's Vintage Garden); glass button and other buttons; embroidery floss; baker's twine; thread; fabric adhesive; sewing needle; scissors

Assemblage Charm

Canvas fabric; burlap; wool roving; lace (Laura's Vintage Garden); chandelier bead; pearl bead chain; two buttons in graduated sizes; three copper eyelets; jump rings; embroidery floss; fabric adhesive; hot glue sticks; hot glue gun; sewing needle; scissors; pliers; needle-felting pen; brush needle-felting pad; Crop-A-Dile (We R Memory Keepers)

Monochromatic Background

5" × 7" (13cm × 18cm) canvas; crocheted doilies; fabric flower, pom-pom trim (Maya Road); lace trim (Laura's Vintage Garden); beads; buttons; letter stamps (Studio G); wax paper; computer paper; black archival ink; gesso; fabric adhesive; paintbrush; scissors; quilting iron

Dahlia From Quilt Scraps

5" × 5" (13cm × 13cm) canvas panel; quilt scraps; fabric; earring; cardboard; fabric adhesive; hot glue sticks; hot glue gun; 1¾" (4cm) circle punch; scissors; petal patterns

Printed Muslin

Oval plate; black-and-white photograph; muslin; crocheted doilies; lace (Laura's Vintage Garden); linen heart, burlap trim, paper posies (Maya Road); buttons; earrings; seam binding; patterned paper; computer paper; alphabet and number stickers; embroidery floss; black thread; ink (Vintage Photo Distress Ink by Ranger); fabric adhesive; clear tape; scissors; pinking shears; laser printer; sewing machine

Fabric Yo-Yos

7" × 9" (18cm × 23cm) canvas; 5" × 7" (13cm × 18cm) canvas; fabric scraps; buttons; lace (Laura's Vintage Garden); charm (Vintaj); embroidery floss; acrylic paint; thick adhesive tape (Stamp Straight Tape by ImpressArt); fabric adhesive; paper towel; sewing needle; yo-yo maker; scissors; metal stamps (ImpressArt); bench block; brass hammer

Pattern Tissue Skirt

3" × 3" (8cm × 8cm) canvas; sewing pattern tissue; patterned paper; muslin; seam binding; bottle cap, wooden button, chandelier beads, fabric trim, chipboard heart (Maya Road); buttons; flower charm (Vintaj); glass E beads; 2" (5cm) wooden disc; milk cap; transfer decal (Nunn Design); wings (Studio 490 by Wendy Vecchi); five screw eyes; jump rings; 16-gauge copper wire; metal foil tape (Ranger); paper clay; glitter; embroidery floss; paints in tan, black and white; ink (Vintage Photo Distress Ink by Ranger); black archival ink; strong liquid adhesive; fabric adhesive; adhesive foam dots; dimensional adhesive (Diamond Glaze by JudiKins); sandpaper; alphabet stamps (Studio G); sewing needle; paintbrush; paper trimmer; scissors; pinking shears; wire cutters; pliers; craft knife; cutting mat; paper piercer

Fabric Wrap

Metal frame lamp shade with outer covering removed; frames and glass (Ranger); pearl bead chain, chandelier beads, key (Maya Road); doilies (Laura's Vintage Garden); spoon; perfume bottle; candy molds; buttons; dried flower; jump rings; fabric; embroidery floss; patterned paper; fabric adhesive; scissors; needle-nose pliers; two-hole punch (ImpressArt)

Chapter Two

Wire Skirt

Bisque doll head (Etsy); two gelatin molds; clear zipper holder; rhinestone trim, large daisy trim, small wooden spool, crystal pin (Maya Road); fabric leaves (Laura's Vintage Garden); wooden spool; plastic cylinder; fabric scrap; seam binding; shell buttons; clear beads; white beads; self-adhesive pearls (The Paper Studio); 24-gauge wire; embroidery floss; strong liquid adhesive; fabric adhesive; scissors; wire cutters; needle-nose pliers

Faux Gold

Cigarette tin; cardboard; small metal tin, chipboard letters, rhinestone trim (Maya Road); lace, flowers, doilies (Laura's Vintage Garden); fractured doll (Advantus); shell buttons; rhinestone brooch; earring; string of pearls; patterned paper; image printed with a laser printer; silver glass glitter; embossing ink; embossing powder; natural beeswax (Ranger); silver ink; silver acrylic paint; seam binding; embroidery floss; thread; adhesive foam dot; fabric adhesive; dimensional adhesive (Diamond Glaze by JudiKins); clothespin; tweezers; paper trimmer; scissors; wire cutters; quilting iron; heat tool

Faux Tintype

5"×7"(13cm×18cm) gallery-wrapped canvas; copper sheeting; copper tape; patterned paper; image and text printed with a laser printer; computer paper; black acrylic paint; gold paint; crackle paint (Clear Rock Candy by Ranger); ink (Vintage Photo Distress Ink by Ranger); matte medium; adhesive foam dots; paper towel; paintbrush; embossing folder (Book Cover by Sizzix); embossing

machine; metal stamps (ImpressArt); scissors; craft knife; cutting mat; bench block; brass hammer

Riveted Patchwork

5"×5"(13cm × 13cm) gallery-wrapped canvas; chipboard heart (Studio 490 by Wendy Vecchi); metal foil tape (Ranger); alcohol ink (Cranberry and Mushroom by Ranger); black acrylic paint; crackle paint (Clear Rock Candy by Ranger); ink (Vintage Photo Distress Ink by Ranger); black gel pen; patterned paper; paper towel; adhesive foam dots; steel wool; ballpoint pen; stylus; paintbrush; scissors; paper trimmer; felt pad and blending tool; scallop border punch (Fiskars)

Faux Mercury Glass

Two 3"×3"(8cm×8cm) canvases; two pieces 2"×2" (5cm×5cm) memory glass (Ranger); glass vial, chipboard heart, doilies, paper posies (Maya Road); beads; earring; quilt scraps; button; baker's twine; seam binding; ribbon (optional); patterned paper; image; paper towel; charcoal pencil; gesso; ink (Jet Black Archival and Vintage Photo Distress Ink by Ranger); Looking Glass mirror spray paint (Krylon); fabric adhesive; clear-drying adhesive; paintbrush; clear stamps (Antiquated Collection by Pink Persimmon); mist bottle filled with water; scissors; pinking shears

Soda Can Flowers

4"×4"(10cm×10cm) gallery-wrapped canvas; two empty aluminum cans; rhinestone buttons; clear bead; patterned paper; transfer decals (Nunn Design); charcoal pencil; cream and aqua acrylic paints; white enamel paint (Ranger); ink (Vintage Photo Distress Ink by Ranger); matte medium; hot glue sticks; hot glue gun; sandpaper; strong adhesive tape; paintbrush; tin snips; blending tool with felt pad; die (Flowers, 3-D Wrapped by Sizzix); embossing folder (Polka Dots by Provo Craft); embossing machine

Assemblage Necklace

Butter knife; pearl bead chain; pearl bead chain with crystals; chandelier bead; self-adhesive pearls (The Paper Studio); two jump rings; 20-gauge wire; rhinestone button with shank; tweezers; hacksaw; drill; jewelry pliers; wire cutters

Stamped Metal

7"×9"(18cm×23cm) canvas; tart tin; light reflector; milk bottle top; muslin; twine; button; beads; bottle; metal charm (Vintaj); jump rings; 16-gauge wire; thread; patterned paper (Pink Paislee); paper towel; ink (Jet Black Archival and Vintage Photo Distress Ink by Ranger); black acrylic paint; fabric adhesive; thick tape (Stamp Straight Tape by ImpressArt); strong liquid adhesive; rubber stamps (Studio G); scissors; paper trimmer; wire cutters; metal stamps, bench block, brass hammer (ImpressArt); sewing machine

Thimble Charm

2" × 3" (5cm × 8cm) canvas; metal thimble; molded doll (page 73); watch face; butterfly charm; paper posies, wooden button, pearl bead chain, rhinestone trim, glass vial (Maya Road); metal foil tape (Ranger); art modeling film (Studio 490 by Wendy Vecchi); two screw eyes; 16-gauge wire; muslin; seam binding; embroidery floss; patterned paper (Pink Paislee); word printed onto paper; transfer decal (Nunn Design); sandpaper; glass glitter; ink (Vintage Photo Distress Ink by Ranger); tan, metallic gold, green acrylic paint; strong liquid adhesive; clear-drying adhesive; butterfly punch (EK Success); paintbrush; scissors; pinking shears; wire cutters; needle-nose pliers; drill

Photo Transfer Onto Metal

Wooden pants hanger; metal tin; metal spoons; mini cake tin; buttons; pearl bead chain (Maya Road); rhinestones; charms (Vintaj); glass bottle (Advantus); screw eyes; glass glitter; muslin; patterned paper (Pink Paislee); images printed with a laser printer; ink (Vintage Photo Distress Ink by Ranger); matte medium; fabric adhesive; paintbrush; mist bottle filled with water; scissors; needle-nose pliers; hammer; heat tool, optional; brayer; metal stamps, bench press, brass hammer, two-hole punch (ImpressArt); drill

Chapter Three

Objects Embedded in Beeswax

2" × 3" (5cm × 8cm) canvas; rhinestone trim (Maya Road); flowers (Laura's Vintage Garden); shell buttons; wooden spool; quilt scraps; feather; seam binding; dried flower; milk cap; microbeads; cardboard; patterned paper; images and words printed with a laser printer; baker's twine; natural beeswax pellets (Ranger); beeswax crayons (Faber-Castell); strong liquid adhesive; tweezers; paper trimmer; scissors; wire cutters; heat tool; quilting iron; house patterns

Wax Engraving

5" × 5" (13cm × 13cm) gallery-wrapped canvas; patterned paper; image printed with a laser printer; paper doily; natural beeswax pellets (Ranger); beeswax crayons (Faber-Castell); pearlescent powdered pigments (Turquoise, Perfect Pearl,

Berry Twist, Sunflower Sparkle, Heirloom Gold Perfect Pearls by Ranger); stylus; paintbrush; rubber stamp; stencil; heart paper punch (Fiskars); quilting iron; heat tool

Molded Embellishments

Item from which to create mold; cardboard frame (7Gypsies); flower trim, rhinestone trim (Maya Road); leaves (Laura's Vintage Garden); buttons; self-adhesive pearls (The Paper Studio); twine; seam binding; patterned paper; glitter glue (Platinum, Diamond Stickles by Ranger); pearlescent pigment powder (Perfect Pearls by Ranger); ink (Vintage Photo Distress Ink by Ranger); strong liquid adhesive; clear and white ultra-thick embossing enamel, two-part molding putty (ETI Enviro-Tex); nonstick craft sheet; rubber spatula; oval paper punch (Fiskars); scallop scissors; heavy-duty hole punch (Crop-A-Dile by We R Memory Keepers); melting pot; heat tool

Faux Glass Tiles

8" × 8" (20cm × 20cm) canvas; cardboard; patterned paper; broken colored glass; lace, floral spray (Laura's Vintage Garden); ribbon; thread; gold-leafing pen; modeling paste (Studio 490 by Wendy Vecchi); clear ultrathick embossing enamel, two-part molding putty (Ranger); stains (Vintage Photo, Wild Honey, Old Paper by Ranger); ink (Vintage Photo Distress Ink by Ranger); crackle paint (Rock Candy by Ranger); dimensional adhesive (Diamond Glaze by JudiKins); strong liquid adhesive; stamps (Studio 490 by Wendy Vecchi); tweezers; palette knife; scissors; melting pot

Clay Flowers

3" × 3" (8cm × 8cm) canvas; chipboard scalloped square (Maya Road); lace; paper doily; patterned paper; sandpaper; chandelier bead (Maya Road); 16-gauge wire; polymer clay; acrylic paint; metallic effects ink (Peacock, Chocolate, Pearl, Gold, Copper by JudiKins); glitter glue (Diamond Stickles by Ranger); inks (Spiced Marmalade, Vintage Photo Distress Ink by Ranger); matte medium; strong liquid adhesive; hot glue sticks; hot glue gun; texture mat (JudiKins); paintbrush; wire cutters; craft knife; cutting mat; heavy-duty hole punch (Crop-A-Dile by We R Memory Keepers); pasta machine or brayer; oven; circle templates in three sizes

Clay Embellishments

4" × 4" (10cm × 10cm) canvas; 3" × 3" (8cm × 8cm) canvas; polymer clay; gesso; metallic effects ink (Peacock, Chocolate, Pearl, Gold, Candy Apple Red, Copper by JudiKins); acrylic paint; inks (Peacock and Vintage Photo Distress Ink by Ranger); embossing ink; clear embossing powder; metal foil tape (Ranger); gel pen; strong liquid adhesive; texture mat (JudiKins); paper punches (EK Success and Fiskars); metal stamps (ImpressArt); stylus; paintbrush; craft knife; nonstick craft sheet (Ranger); heat tool; pasta machine or brayer; oven

Faux Enamel

Metal spoon, flattened; leaf charm (Vintaj); two jump rings; assorted beads; microbeads (Copper, Florentine Gold, Sterling by EK Success); acrylic paint; embossing powders (Malachite, Egyptian Gold, Metallic Copper, Metallic Gold by JudiKins); enameling resin (Fluxe by JudiKins); copper sheeting; strong liquid adhesive; heat-resistant nonstick craft sheet, nonstick craft sheet (Ranger); metal stamps, bench block, brass hammer (ImpressArt); melting pot; drill

Resin Charm

Charm bracelet chain, shield pendant (Nunn Design); other charms (Nunn Design, Vintaj); rhinestone trim (Maya Road); beads; buttons; jump rings; two-part resin (ETI EnviroTex Resin); transfer decal (Nunn Design); acrylic paint; thick tape (Stamp Straight Tape by ImpressArt); dimensional adhesive, optional (Diamond Glaze by JudiKins); disposable gloves; disposable mixing cup; craft stick; bowl with water; paint-brush; tweezers; wire cutters; pliers; scissors; metal stamps, bench block, brass hammer (ImpressArt); heat tool or plastic straw (optional)

Faux Porcelain Flowers

Paper flowers and leaves; wooden spool; doily (Laura's Vintage Garden); copper disk (ImpressArt); jump ring; memo clip (Advantus); muslin; embroidery floss; patterned paper; printed sentiment; nonstick craft sheet, clear ultra-thick embossing enamel (Ranger); black acrylic paint; black ink; hot glue sticks; hot glue gun; fabric adhesive; stamp (Antiquated Collection by Pink Persimmon); scissors; pliers; metal stamps, bench block, brass hammer, two-hole punch (ImpressArt); melting pot

Jewelry Clay Butterfly

2" × 3" (5cm × 8cm) canvas; chipboard butterfly (Maya Road); silver microbeads (EK Success); beads; buttons; cuff links; rhinestones; resin flower; patterned paper; crackle paint (Clear Rock Candy by Ranger); black acrylic paint; ink (Vintage Photo Distress Ink by Ranger); pearlescent pigment powder (Biscotti Perfect Pearls by Ranger); jewelry clay (ETI EnviroTex Resin); strong liquid adhesive; disposable gloves; paintbrush; bowl; tweezers

Chapter Four

Paper Feather

4" × 4" (10cm × 10cm) canvas; shell buttons; thin patterned paper; seam binding; embroidery floss; glass glitter; crackle paint (Clear Rock Candy by Ranger); acrylic paint (Snow Cap, Shell Pink, Juniper by Ranger); ink (Jet Black Archival and Vintage Photo Distress Ink by Ranger); pearlescent pigment powder (Blush Perfect Pearls by Ranger); modeling paste (Studio 490 by Wendy Vecchi); floral wire; glitter glue (Diamond, Platinum Stickles by Ranger); strong liquid adhesive; matte medium; adhesive foam dots; charcoal pencil; pencil; alphabet stamps; stencil (Studio 490 Wendy Vecchi); paintbrush; paper trimmer; scissors; wire cutters; feather pattern

Accented Papers

5" × 7" (13cm × 18cm) canvas; scalloped chipboard, chipboard pieces (including one 1½" × 1½" [4cm × 4cm] piece), wooden ruler, skeleton key, bingo motif, bingo calendar, crystal trinket pin, heart pin, brown velvet blossom, rhinestone trim (Maya Road); glass bottle, clock key (Advantus); metal edging (Studio 490 by Wendy Vecchi); metal buttons; shell buttons; beads; dried roses; game pieces; feather; pearl pin (Jenni Bowlin Studio); burlap; seam binding; self-adhesive pearls (The Paper Studio); patterned paper; jewelry tag (American Tag Company); embroidery floss; gold and black acrylic paint; ink (Jet Black Archival and Black Soot, Vintage Photo Distress Ink by Ranger); crackle paint (Clear Rock Candy by Ranger); silver ink pen; glitter glue (Diamond Stickles by Ranger); glue stick; strong liquid adhesive; dimensional adhesive (Glossy Accents by Ranger); adhesive foam dots; stamps (Antiquated Collection by Pink Persimmon); acrylic block; paper trimmer; scissors; craft knife; cutting mat

Photo Silhouette

4" × 4" (10cm × 10cm) canvas; adhesive canvas (Sticky Back Canvas by Ranger); patterned paper (Jenni Bowlin Studio); black cardstock; image of person or people; tissue tape (Vintage Paper by Advantus); metal foil tape (Ranger); black ink (Jet Black Archival by Ranger); strong liquid adhesive; adhesive foam dots; pencil; alphabet stamps (Studio G); scissors; decorative scissors; craft knife; cutting mat; stylus; mist bottle filled with water

Charms From Vintage Papers

1" (3cm) wooden square; metal jewelry bail (The Paper Studio); rhinestone button; pearl bead chain; jump rings; image; computer paper; ink; gold-leafing pen; two-part resin (ETI EnviroTex Resin); disposable mixing cups; craft stick; aluminum metal foil tape (Ranger); sandpaper; glue stick; clear-drying glue; E6000; scissors; pinking shears; laser printer

Canvas Paper Transfer

Chipboard frame and trim (Studio 490 by Wendy Vecchi); chipboard flower; chipboard letters; adhesive canvas (Sticky Back Canvas by Ranger); patterned paper (Pink Paislee); embossing ink; embossing powder (Clear and Egyptian Gold by JudiKins); ink (Jet Black Archival and Peacock, Vintage Photo Distress Ink by Ranger); green acrylic paint; crackle paint (Tattered Rose, Fired Brick, Shabby Shutters by Ranger); glitter glue (Diamond, Rock Candy Stickles by Ranger); matte medium; strong liquid adhesive; adhesive foam dots; paper towel; stamps (Studio 490 by Wendy Vecchi); mist bottle filled with water; acrylic block; blending tool; brayer; scissors; heat tool; bird die (Sizzix); die cut machine

Faux Resin Leaves

4" x 12" (10cm x 30cm) canvas; buttons; patterned paper; aluminum can; 16-gauge wire; embroidery floss; gesso; tan, green, aqua acrylic paint; black ink (Jet Black Archival by Ranger); coarse glitter; steel wool; matte medium; clear-drying adhesive; dimensional adhesive (Diamond Glaze by JudiKins); hot glue sticks; hot glue gun; straight pin; paint-brush; stamp (Antiquated Collection by Pink Persimmon); flower punch (EK Success); tweezers; scissors; wire cutters; craft knife; cutting mat

Patchwork Background

4" x 4" (10cm x 10cm) gallery-wrapped canvas; Grungepaper (Advantus); patterned paper; computer paper; acrylic paint; ink (Vintage Photo Distress Ink by Ranger); thread; pearlescent pigment powder in three colors (Perfect Pearls by Ranger); gold marker; paper towel; sandpaper; tape runner; strong liquid adhesive; paintbrush; paper trimmer; scissors; butterfly die, embossing folder (Provo Craft); embossing machine; metal stamps, bench block, brass hammer (ImpressArt); sewing machine

Resin Paper

4" x 4" (10cm x 10cm) canvas; chipboard butterfly (Maya Road); molded doll; patterned paper (Pink Paislee); printed

sentiment; self-adhesive pearls; two-part resin (ETI EnviroTex Resin); ink (Jet Black Archival and Vintage Photo Distress Ink by Ranger); tan acrylic paint; coarse glitter (EK Success); thread; matte medium; strong liquid adhesive; plastic wrap; sandpaper; disposable gloves; disposable mixing cup; craft stick; disposable paintbrush; stamp (Antiquated Collection by Pink Persimmon); butterfly punch (EK Success); acrylic block; tweezers; scissors; sewing machine

Decoupage Papier-Mâché

5" x 7" (13cm x 18cm) canvas; papier-mâché bird (EK Success); pearl bead chain, chandelier bead, metal key (Maya Road); two jump rings; buttons; paper doily; patterned paper (Pink Paislee); chipboard or Grungepaper (Advantus); sewing pattern tissue; sentiment printed on paper; baker's twine; seam binding; thread; green and gold acrylic paint; ink (Vintage Photo Distress Ink by Ranger); glitter glue (Diamond Stickles by Ranger); matte medium; strong liquid adhesive; charcoal pencil; paintbrushes; stamp (Pink Persimmon); scallop scissors; pinking shears; scissors; pliers; metal stamps, bench block, brass hammer (ImpressArt); embossing folder (Provo Craft); embossing machine; sewing machine

Spool Tassel

2" x 3" (5cm x 8cm) gallery-wrapped canvas; chipboard butterfly, chipboard silhouette, wooden spool, pearl bead chain (Maya Road); 20-gauge wire; three screw eyes; patterned paper; stamped sentiment; seam binding in three colors; sandpaper; modeling paste (Studio 490 by Wendy Vecchi); embossing ink, clear embossing powder (Ranger); ink (Jet Black Archival and Vintage Photo Distress Ink by Ranger); black acrylic paint; crackle paint (Clear Rock Candy by Ranger); pearlescent pigment powder (Copper, Biscotti Perfect Pearls by Ranger); glitter glue (Stickles by Ranger); strong liquid adhesive; dimensional adhesive (Diamond Glaze by JudiKins); adhesive foam dots; hot glue sticks; hot glue gun; paintbrush; stencil (The Crafter's Workshop); stamps (Studio G); paper trimmer; scissors; wire cutters; needle-nose pliers; heat tool

Resources

The following companies manufacture products featured in this book. Please check your local retailers to find these materials, or go to the company's website for the latest product information.

7Gypsies
www.sevengypsies.com

American Tag Company
www.americantag.net

Collage Stuff
www.collagestuff.com

The Crafter's Workshop
www.thecraftersworkshop.com

DMC
www.dmc-usa.com

EK Success
www.eksuccessbrands.com

Enviromental Technology Inc.
www.eti-usa.com

Faber-Castell
www.fabercastell.com

Fiskars
www3.fiskars.com

ILoveToCreate
www.ilovetocreate.com

ImpressArt
www.impressart.com

Jenni Bowlin Studio
www.jbsmercantile.com

JudiKins
www.judikins.com

Krylon
www.krylon.com

Laura's Vintage Garden
www.etsy.com/shop/laurasvintage-garden

Maya Road, LLC
www.mayaroad.net

Nunn Design
www.nunndesign.com

The Paper Studio
www.paperstudio.com

Pink Paislee
www.pinkpaislee.com

Pink Persimmon
www.pinkpersimmon.com

Provo Craft
www.provocraft.com

Ranger Industries, Inc.
www.rangerink.com

Sizzix
www.sizzix.com

Studio 490 by Wendy Vecchi
www.stampersanonymous.com

Studio G
www.hamptonart.com

Tim Holtz idea-ology
www.timholtz.com/prod_cat/idea-ology-products

Vintaj
www.vintaj.com

We R Memory Keepers
www.weronthenet.com

Xyron
www.xyron.com

Index

About the Author

Lisa Pace loves all things that sparkle, show dimension and look vintage. Her first memory of creating a project was as a three-year-old child, sitting at the kitchen table with her mom. From then on, she devoted her life to honing her skills as a mixed-media artist. Her most recent artistic outlet has been papercrafting. Since 2005, she has had numerous items published in magazines and idea books. Lisa's highly popular technique-based books *Delight in the Details* and *Delight in the Seasons* were published in 2010 and 2012. In 2011, Lisa collaborated with Pink Persimmon and released her vintage-inspired stamp line Antiquated Collection. Lisa enjoys teaching a variety of mixed-media classes and workshops in the United States and abroad.

Lisa's work is marked by her ability to rethink and reuse. Her commitment to always add that special embellishment sets her work apart from others. She says that the heart of her designs is "in the details." Lisa currently lives in Frisco, Texas, with her husband.

To learn more about Lisa, visit her at www.lisapace.com.

Dedication

To my husband, Alan, and daughters, Terri and Ansley. You three have always believed in and encouraged me in my artful ventures, and for this I'm truly grateful. You have accepted that the kitchen table and all other flat surfaces around the house will always be covered in art supplies and flea market finds. And you overlook that I'm better at heating beeswax and assembling art than cooking and preparing dinner.

I love you truly.

Acknowledgments

I want to thank everyone at F+W Media, Inc. and North Light Books for putting so much of their time and energy into creating this book. I know this never would have come to be without all of your behind-the-scenes work and dedication. Thank you.

Special thanks to my editors Kristy Conlin and Christine Doyle and photographer Christine Polomsky. I feel so fortunate to once again get to work with you. You three are amazing.

Caroline, Ronda and Wendy, I am forever grateful for your years of friendship and support. You always keep it honest and real. Thank you for accepting me for who I am—a creative, quirky, type-A personality artist who has the attention span of a gnat.

Special thanks to iLoveToCreate, a Duncan Enterprises Company, and Xyron for generously donating the adhesives I used on projects in this book.

Thank you to these wonderful companies who so generously donated their products: The Crafty Scrapper, ETI EnviroTex Resin, Fiskars, iLoveToCreate—a Duncan Enterprises Company, ImpressArt, Jenni Bowlin Studio, JudiKins, Laura's Vintage Garden, Maya Road, Nunn Design, Pink Paislee, Pink Persimmon, Ranger Ink, Studio 490 by Wendy Vecchi ~ Stampers Anonymous, Tim Holtz idea-ology, Vintaj and Xyron.

Metric Conversion Chart		
To convert	to	multiply by
Inches	Centimeters	2.54
Centimeters	Inches	0.4
Feet	Centimeters	30.5
Centimeters	Feet	0.03
Yards	Meters	0.9
Meters	Yards	1.1

18 17 16 15 14   5 4 3 2 1

ISBN 978-1-4403-2853-4

DISTRIBUTED IN CANADA BY FRASER DIRECT
100 Armstrong Avenue
Georgetown, ON, Canada L7G 5S4
Tel: (905) 877-4411

DISTRIBUTED IN THE U.K. AND EUROPE
BY F&W MEDIA INTERNATIONAL, LTD
Brunel House, Forde Close, Newton Abbot, TQ12 4PU, UK
Tel: (+44) 1626 323200, Fax: (+44) 1626 323319
Email: enquiries@fwmedia.com

DISTRIBUTED IN AUSTRALIA BY CAPRICORN LINK
P.O. Box 704, S. Windsor NSW, 2756 Australia
Tel: (02) 4560-1600, Fax: (02) 4577-5288
Email: books@capricornlink.com.au

Edited by Kristy Conlin and Christine Doyle
Designed by Amanda Kleiman
Production coordinated by Greg Nock
Photography by Christine Polomsky and Kris Kandler

Add More Delight to Your Day!

We have even more FREE *Delight in the Art of Collage* companion content to inspire you! Just go to:

ArtistsNetwork.com/delight-collage

for access to bonus materials and printable templates.

Easy Mixed Media Surface Techniques
Seth Apter
NORTH LIGHT DVD | an artistsnetwork.tv production

COLLAGE CRAFTS GONE WILD
Mixed-media projects and techniques
FEATURING PROJECTS FROM
Traci Bautista, Claudine Hellmuth, Kelly Rae Roberts and more!

our 50TH ISSUE
CELEBRATE FALL WITH PRINTMAKING
cloth paper scissors
COLLAGE MIXED MEDIA | ARTISTIC DISCOVERY
TRY 2 unique ENCAUSTIC TECHNIQUES
Meet cover artist LOUISE O'HARA
add TEXTURE with heat & glazes

These and other fine North Light mixed media products are available from your local art and craft retailer, bookstore and favorite online supplier. Visit our websites at **ArtistsNetwork.com** and **ArtistsNetwork.tv**.

Follow North Light Books for the latest news, free wallpapers, free demos and chances to win FREE BOOKS!

Visit artistsnetwork.com and get Jen's North Light Picks!

Get free step-by-step demonstrations along with reviews of the latest books, videos and downloads from Jennifer Lepore, Senior Editor and Online Education Manager at North Light Books.

Jen's PICKS

Get involved

Learn from the experts. Join the conversation on:

WetCanvas

128